Materialism and Dialectics in Post-classical World

Impact of Electromagnetism

Anil Rajimwale

AAKAR

Materialism and Dialectics in Post-classical World:
Impact of Electromagnetism
Anil Rajimwale

First Published 2021

ISBN 978-93-5002-670-0

Published by
AAKAR BOOKS
28 E Pocket IV, Mayur Vihar Phase I
Delhi 110 091 India
aakarbooks@gmail.com

Laser Typeset at
Arpit Printographers, Delhi

Printed at
Sapra Brothers, Noida

Contents

Introduction

Electromagnetism (EM) and its impact on our worldview and philosophy is the main object of our study in this book. Electromagnetism is something transitional between the tangible and the intangible worlds, connecting the two, inaugurating the intangible world, and thus a new world reality, which may be termed as post-classical. Thus it is a transition from the classical to post-classical world. Therefore it demands a transition from the classical worldview to a post-classical one. EM links the tangible and the intangible. The transition brings to us the concrete problems of how to give up old and outdated methods and to adopt the new ones based on new vantage points.

This stepping into a post-classical world presents us with fresh philosophical problems. Problems of philosophy which seemed settled have emerged anew, demanding solutions with growing force. We need fresh generalizations, and therefore fresh philosophy or fresh approaches to philosophical questions. Thus the EM launches us both into the new concrete realities as well as propels us towards novel philosophical solutions. The build up of the classical age breaks down.

Atom and atomism have been under severe stress for the past century or so. The atom not only got divided, it has opened a whole new world, where it simply does not exist! This has given rise to speculations of all sorts, including of 'disappearance', 'death' and 'overthrow' of matter. The end of atom has created problems as to what constitutes the new reality, where waves, particles and exceedingly rapid motions rule without limits.

Innumerable other 'atoms' and 'particles' have been discovered in the interval. The division has now reached a qualitative point, where the very existence of particle is threatened: the moment you try to observe or 'touch' the particle, it is transformed into waves and so on. Observation of the reality has become problematic. A serious crisis has engulfed the worldview and the process of cognition.

Electromagnetism has completed the break-up of the atom, and has filled the inter-stellar space with its ever-deepening contents. Space between planets and stars are full of endless activities/events of waves, particles, fields, energy and rapid conversions of a post-classical nature. The post-classical particle has replaced the classical atom.

Our worldview and perceptions are products of the classical age, dominated by industrial revolution. Our life and ways, views and attitudes have been shaped by a world full of tangible objects and their motions; thoughts, consciousness and philosophy have been fashioned by what we have seen with our own eyes, both on the earth and out into the space. The world for us is full of objects of various shapes, sizes and qualities. We are habituated to such a reality. Our conclusions about the unseen and the micro-reality too are based on the workings of the tangible world.

The industrial revolution caused a leap in our thought by providing qualitatively new tools of knowledge like the steam engine-driven machines, mills and factories, means of transport, various equipments and gadgets like telescope and microscope, modern physical and chemical laboratories, diesel and electricity-driven machines and so on. Natural sciences, as also the social sciences, helped us penetrate deep into matter and its mechanics. The sciences studied various fields of reality, unfolding the inner workings and motions of numerous kinds.

Today, as we enter the post-industrial, postmodern and electronics age, the worldview and philosophy is under severe stress and crisis, pressing for fundamental change. It is a revolution of higher order, creating a post-classical era based upon forces and processes unnatural for us, forces not occurring naturally. We are not used to the workings of electrons, photons, protons and such other forces. Electronics though has made a big inroad in form of the computers and the mobiles. We are certainly not used to the workings of the quantum forces.

It is only now that they have begun to impact our consciousness.

The human being has evolved in natural planetary conditions of the earth. Our brain has also evolved precisely in such conditions, and therefore is not used to the unnatural conditions or conditions not naturally occurring. With the unleashing of forces within the atom, a deepening crisis of thought and philosophy has set in. The dividing lines between the object and the subject, between matter and idea, are getting blurred. New and unprecedented aspects of matter are being revealed, creating problems for cognition. This can broadly be characterized as part of a post-industrial, postmodern consciousness. Let it be clear that this postmodernism is different from the concepts currently being expressed as 'postmodernism', by the postmodernist schools of thought.

Understanding EM is the first major step to fashion new thought-process and new consciousness.

Anil Rajimwale

1

Atom and Atomism

It was industrial revolution which *actually* discovered atoms and particles, *hypothesized* by the entire previous human history. Atomism is an age-old *concept*, developed since ancient times, to explain nature of the world. Democritus of Miletus in Greece in 5th century BC is credited with being the originator of the *concept of atomism*. Perhaps his master Leucippus also had a hand in the discovery. Atomism is the notion that there is the smallest indivisible part, atom, from which the universe and everything in it is formed.[1] If you go on dividing anything, we will ultimately reach the smallest indivisible 'atom'.

Democritus said that everything is composed of atoms, between atoms lies the empty space, atoms are indestructible, and they have always been and will be in motion. For different kinds of materials (elements) there are different kinds of atoms.[2] For example, the atoms of iron have hooks, while those of water are smooth.

Points of view of Leucippus and Democritus were remarkably like those of the modern science, and avoided most of the faults of Greek speculation.[3]

The atomists agreed that atoms required void in between. Parmenides said: "You say there *is* void; therefore void is not nothing. Therefore there is not the void." "Democritus was a thorough-going materialist; for him… the soul was composed of atoms, and thought was a physical process. There was no purpose in the universe; there were only atoms governed by mechanical laws."[4]

"Epicurus was a materialist, but not a determinist. He followed Democritus in believing that the world consists of atoms and the void; but he did not believe, as Democritus did, that the atoms are at all times completely controlled by natural laws." His atoms had weight, falling downwards in an absolute sense.[5]

The contribution of Democritus is brilliantly established by Karl Marx in his PhD theses on "Difference between the Democritean and Epicurean Philosophy of Nature in General."[6] He also mentions the contribution of Leucippus in it.

Marx deals in detail with the concepts of atom in Democritus and Epicurus. It is a fascinating comparison, the contrast and unity between the two. Generalizing from their approaches, Marx says that in them "the *atom* is the *immediate negation of abstract space,* hence a spatial point."[7]

The *atom has been a powerful tool of philosophy throughout the history to explain the world,* and therefore is a key to both materialist and idealist worldviews. It has held its ground from the ancient times till today. Discoveries of modern sciences and inventions of technologies and tools helped concretize the hypothesis of atomism, the reality of atom and evolve the concept of matter. The atoms in this worldview have been treated more like the tangible objects, existing in time and space, and in motion following Newtonian laws. They are comparable to any tangible bodies existing on the earth and in the skies.

Industrial View of World

The industrial world is characterized by orderly placing of objects and their motions in time and space. In the natural sciences, physics and philosophy, it is known as the *Newtonian* or *Cartesian* (named so after the name of Descartes and his ideas) world. Human society and consciousness have so far evolved in a Cartesian/Newtonian ambience. These are scientific terms of a particular origin, yet they are applicable in general to describe the classical and modern reality. We will have the occasion later to discuss 'reality', the concept of which has been shaken by the recent developments in electromagnetism, quantum mechanics and relativity.

Railways, modern roads and industrial steam ships helped us penetrate the world around us. We went to the unknown areas, lands, seas, oceans, continents, hills, mountains, forests, poles and so on, discovering ever new aspects of reality, leading to ever expanding knowledge. Railways continue to amaze us even today, both young and old, by unfolding ever new realities. Merchants and scientists visited new geographical areas. Darwin not only discovered new lands, he discovered evolution of life-forms in ascending order of growing complexity, leading ultimately to the discovery of origins of human beings from apes, and consolidated our philosophical view of world in motion. Galileo and Newton before him provided a view of the mechanical motions of the heavenly and earthly bodies.

Modern machines introduced us to the mechanical and repetitive motion containing its own dialectics. This dialectics was covered in mechanical and metaphysical cover. To uncover dialectics of mechanical motion, we have to follow step by step the complicated series of study of reality and concepts. We needed philosophy and worldview to understand the relations between us and the world in circulation round us. Machines led us to interpret the motion of atoms in mechanical, physical and chemical manner. Atoms joined together to constitute elements, compounds and inorganic/organic realities. The thought that the world was constituted of atoms was confirmed, their motions assimilated, becoming inalienable part of our consciousness.

In all this, we needed increasingly complicated tools, equipments and gadgets.

Thus the modern human being and consciousness are basically product of industrial revolution. Consciousness of objects and of their motions all around us is part and parcel of our life. We manipulate and use objects for daily use. We have so many things around us: stones, rocks, trees, cars, roads, railways, machines, tools, growing number of houses and buildings, endless commodities, which all have their own role in expanding our consciousness and activities in a particular way: they are tangibly clear and well-ordered. We have roads, railways, fly-over, transport which take us to new realities constituted by modern development. We see ever new realities and make ever new discoveries constituted by their motions.

Our view of space, time and the objects therein is composed of the clear and tangible objects and their motions, both slow and fast. We are habituated and attuned to these motions, and are fashioned by them in turn. Even our ideal world is the reflection of these material/tangible motions, which have created the human being down the ages.

Even our daily routine is in motion, seemingly 'like' an industrial machine. Combination of nature and industrial society determine our life activities. We rise every day to go to our place of work or study. This going and coming back is inextricably determined by the rise and setting of the sun or other sources of light. In our endeavors we tends to extend the sun (light) into our daily life, production, studies, business, etc. A day is constituted by so many activities and motions. Yet one day is no different from the previous one or the next, apparently. One is expected out of the other. Change is discernible only over time.

Our consciousness has discovered the reality of time and space, and their concepts, within which we evolved. Events take place in time and space. We place ourselves and move in certain space and move in certain time intervals. The events belong to the material and ideal worlds, as unity of reality. They have become inalienable part of our consciousness.

Our view of motions (*motion*, philosophically speaking) is

beautiful: we can see them. Things 'move' and grow. Colors for example are very beautiful, causing emanation of feelings: feelings are nothing but complete surrender to the emotions generated by motions. Yet these emotions are incomplete. The industrial beings philosophized about matter, time and space, about motion/s. For the first time philosophy came in direct relationship with objects and things, material forms. Earlier, it was in relation with abstractions, with little actual generalization. Philosophy essentially is generalization and speculation. Industrial revolution, sciences and industrial technologies converted ideal abstractions into material abstractions, into generalizations of the processes of the world.

Industrial revolution was the greatest tool to delve into motions on the earth and outside.

Thus we developed certain worldview and philosophy. The job of scientific philosophy has been to delve into various fields of reality, a job increasingly being discharged by the sciences. To discover inner workings of a phenomenon or process, we have to go deeper and spread out wider with the help of concepts developed by the sciences and so many different philosophical schools. For example discovery of sources of motion is not an easy job, and needs detailed and painstaking study and research into each field.

Natural sciences including physics uncover realities of different aspects matter and reality, enriching consciousness. Sciences, physics and philosophy, as also social studies, overlap in many respects, as far as generalization and philosophy is concerned. Yet they contribute to creation of a unified picture through synthesis.

The recent developments and discoveries in the natural sciences, in particular in physics, have given a jolt to our well-established notions. The events in physics in particular have jolted us out of our age-old worldview, because they have snatched away the vary basis of our thought. The discoveries in this field are spreading socially in form of tools, gadgets, equipments etc.

At the same time, the discoveries are bringing new facts about the reality and its motions and laws.

Here we will be dealing with certain events in physics, crucially in electromagnetism, and trace their impact on our worldview, on the way we look at the world. These events have a deeper and wider impact upon philosophy. Recent discoveries in physics have re-invigorated philosophical debates.

Newton and Worldview

Certain developments took place in the natural sciences, deeply affecting our worldview and philosophical approach. Though philosophy draws from all the branches of knowledge, certain natural sciences like physics, chemistry and biology, physics in particular, are questioning our established notions. This is because physics presently studies, goes deeper into, the microworld, inside the atom, into electromagnetism and the quantum world, a world qualitatively different from the one we live in. Consequently, we are perplexed about *how to look* at the new world.

They also provide us new tools of knowledge. We will be talking about natural sciences, physics and Newtonian motions more because we have to link up with events in sciences further on. In broader sense, 'Newtonian' motion happens in all the fields of mechanical world of machines and their daily usage.

Machines, physics and astronomy provide a general view of the material reality. They are closely related with our daily lives as well as with our views of the objects around us. Immanuel Kant said in a famous comment of his that "two things fill the mind with ever new and increasing admiration and awe... the starry heavens above and the moral law within."[8] "To him the starry heavens were a reminder that the world, as pictured by Hobbes and Newton, is a system of bodies in motion, where every event has a specific and determinate cause."[9]

At present we are not concerned with 'the moral laws within', but it is clear that the ideas of those times were fashioned by the motions around us. Not only Hobbes and Newton but the ideas of other thinkers were also molded and structured largely by the motions of the bodies all around and by the motions of the living beings. These tangible motions shaped the philosophies not only of the two thinkers mentioned above but also of a large body of outstanding philosophers, scientists and observers. The industrial age produced a great number of fine thinkers in a short span of just two or three centuries. The age is called Newtonian, not just because Newton dominated the scientific thought but also because the objective world existing outside and the consequent philosophical thinking was 'Newtonian'. It is a 'Newtonian' world that we have described above. It is also known as 'Cartesian', after Descartes, the famous philosopher.

A host of philosophical schools such as empiricism, rationalism, positivism, materialism, idealism, Marxism, Weberism, and so on emerged out of this terrain. Outstanding thinkers worked out aspects/trends of thought, such as Hobbes, Locke, Spinoza, Descartes, Mill, Spencer, Fichte, Berkeley, Schiller, Hegel, Feuerbach, Marx, Kant and a host of others. They each worked out this or that field/aspect and generalized as philosophy.

Philosophy, Science and Physics

Concepts like matter, idea, reality, existence, causation, object/subject relation, and others are used both in philosophy and physics, as also in other sciences. Besides they have philosophical as well as natural scientific connotations. For example, the concepts like matter and reality are overlapping yet different in many ways in philosophy and physics.

Developments in natural sciences (also in social sciences) have helped develop and strengthened concepts/notions/theories in philosophy. Natural sciences have played a decisive role in enriching philosophical concepts, materialist philosophy in particular. Notions of motion and its laws have stimulated serious controversies in philosophy. New discoveries have led to a crisis in philosophy and in thought in general. Philosophy has become increasingly dependent upon the discoveries in the natural and social sciences for its development.

The great number of discoveries in the natural sciences in the 19th-20th centuries had generated lively controversies regarding concepts of worldview and philosophy: Darwin's evolution of species, laws of conservation and transformation of energy, cellular unity of the living world, Newton's discoveries and theories, Einstein's discoveries, genetics, mechanical laws of gases, laws of mechanical motions, discoveries in astronomy and so on.

While the development of the sciences somewhat diverted the attention from philosophy, it also raised new issues, and strengthened philosophical world outlook. In fact, it will be more correct to state that the sciences took over the functions of philosophy and rendered the latter superfluous. Yet the recent events have raised the philosophical problems afresh, giving rise to debates on basic concepts such as aspects/nature of reality and existence, matter, cause and effect, subjectivity and objectivity, observation, measurement, time, space, and so on. Electromagnetism, quantum, relativity and discoveries in a host of other fields have rekindled philosophical debates.

The events have deeply affected our concept of reality and existence, to the extent that it affects the whole worldview. Questions are being raised as to whether there exists a world 'out there'. Therefore in this book we will be discussing the implications and impact of certain major discoveries in physics, in particular electromagnetism, to the extent they modify our approach to the world/existence itself.

World of 'Newtonian' Motion

According to Einstein, Newton was a brilliant genius who determined the course of western thought "like no one else before or since".[10]

Why should we discuss Newton? Because it was he who discovered the three laws of motion of tangible bodies, the 'heavenly' bodies. He also discovered gravitation. Both his discoveries, and others, guide our daily lives even today and are inseparably intertwined with our consciousness and activities.

What are those three laws? In brief and simplified form, they as follows:

First law: Every body continues to be in a state of rest or uniform motion straight forward, except when it is compelled to change its state by an external force.

Second law: The alteration of motion is proportional to the force applied, and this happens in the direction of the force applied.

Third law: To every action, there is an equal and opposite reaction, or the mutual action of two bodies upon each other are always equal and directed to contrary (the opposite) bodies.

It became clear that the bodies 'interacted at distance'. The bodies, earth, sun, moon, and the stars, objects, spheres, balls, rocks, etc exerted force upon each other even when they were separated, at shorter or longer distances. This led to the law of gravitation.

Newton's laws of motion explain the movement of tangible objects, of which the world is made up. We have been guided and shaped by his laws for more than two hundred years, and they have become part and parcel of our consciousness, without even our realizing it. We assimilate Newton through fashioning machines, raising buildings and structures, running factories and transport, wheels of all kinds, raising infrastructure, digging deeper into the earth, going out into the space, observing planets and stars, etc. Newtonian mechanical motions have become an inalienable part of our consciousness and existence.

A complete chain of physical causation hardly existed before Newton.[11] His object was to trace simple rule through which the motions of heavenly bodies could be explained and calculated. Newton tried to find out how the state of the motion of a system gives rise to that which immediately follows it in time. Newton tried to discover differential law, which satisfies the quest for causality. "The clear conception of the differential law is one of Newton's greatest intellectual achievements."[12] His laws of motion provide an answer to the question related with change of motion (differential law). This is how he reached a conclusion applying to all motions. He connected force and acceleration by introducing the concept of mass.[13]

Scientific and technological events of this age, deeply impacted by the industrial revolution, confirmed the correctness of laws of motion of the tangible bodies.

With the ancient Greeks, the laws of motion were vague and qualitative. The classical world view evolved during 16th to 19th centuries through laws and categories of motion of the existing objects, thus explaining the world. It was a well ordered world based on series of causality. Classical mechanics deals primarily with the motions of bodies through the space. There emerged a tendency in physics and science in general to express the laws in a precise *quantitative* form, culminating in the laws of motion in Newton.[14]

It is interesting to note that the laws of motion discovered by Newton create a particular perception of the world. They help us understand the behavior of the bodies in space and time, and also the nature of the material bodies themselves, which have space and time dimensions. Newton's laws also determine the future behavior of the system of bodies *"completely and precisely for all time"*.[15]

The first known form of mechanism was the philosophy of atomism of Democritus and Leucippus of the ancient Greece. They assumed that "everything in the universe could be reduced to nothing than the effects of motions of atoms through space."[16] The assumption of Laplace was similar in which his determinism also formulated that the behavior of the atoms was governed by the laws of Newton, leading to a precise calculation of the future behavior of the universe.[17]

Consequently, the properties of the atoms are divided into two kinds: those appearing as at large-scale are qualitative and *subjective*, such as hardness, fluidity, color, etc, because they did not appear in *the basic laws of the atoms*. The basic, objective and fundamental properties of the atom are expressed in quantitative terms such as velocity, position, size, shape, mass etc, because they are not the properties of our thinking.[18]

The mechanistic philosophy / view got inspiration from the mechanical nature of the industrial revolution and its machines. The 'machine' became the main source of interpretation of motions found everywhere in the world, and thus created mechanical worldviews, wherein the world was seen as a system working on the pattern of a machine. This included the observations of the processes on the earth, the human body, the solar system and in fact the working of the whole universe. "In this early form of the mechanistic philosophy, the basic elements out of which the world was assumed to be constructed were effectively conceived of as mechanical parts, each of which has its place in a universal machine."[19] This machine is frictionless because according to the laws of classical mechanics, mechanical energy is conserved.

On the one hand, the mechanistic materialist philosophy was a great advance over the scholastic philosophy prevalent during the middle ages. The scholastic philosophy considered every thing and every quality of a thing as separate, eternal and immutable.

The mechanistic philosophy established an *inherent unity*

among the diverse and self-sustained closed systems and parts thereof. This philosophy explained why the processes took place and how did they emerge. Thus a more consistent, unified and dynamic worldview became possible with the mechanistic philosophy.

At the same time, during the mechanical age initiated before the industrial revolution and completed by it, certain developments took place which began to breach the mechanical understanding. Laws of electromagnetism, studies on the motion of gases, statistical explanations for the laws of thermodynamics and other developments took the worldview away from the mechanistic view, to an extent. Initially this needed series of adjustments and revisions, while remaining within the general mechanistic framework. During the classical times, even light was interpreted in Newtonian terms with mechanical action between the light particles. Thus the light particles appeared to behave as any other tangible bodies.

Developments in Sciences and Concept of *Reality*

Certain developments took place in physics towards the end of 19th and the beginning of 20th centuries, which were not 'industrial' and 'mechanical' in nature, bringing about a drastic and qualitative change in the established concepts in philosophy in particular and thought in general. Since the new events were not industrial, they also were not 'orderly' and 'properly arranged' in nature, to which we are used. We began to journey from nature to deeper and wider into nature. It was felt that nature determines 'us' only superficially. In reality it constitutes us by going through us. The new forces that broke up our vision were not natural, they were 'unnatural'.

Physics is a particular field or subject, but it is also studies the wider physical and material reality, and as such helps us develop the concept of 'matter', reality and existence. It often becomes 'non-physical' after a certain level of delving deeper into reality. The *non-physical* is sought to be identified with the 'non-material'. What was taken as granted earlier was shaken to the roots and upset. The process continues still.

The new discoveries have upset the age-old notions about matter and objects, subject-object relationship, objectivity, reality, motion, observation, and so on. They have imparted new meanings to 'observation'. Science, and consequently philosophy, entered new phase, wherein new concepts are needed to explain the world. It became obvious that the established notions were coming in conflict with the new ones, and were unable to explain the new findings about reality and matter. *Classical thought entered a period of deep crisis.*

The new discoveries in physics most of all, as also in other sciences like chemistry, biology etc have raised philosophical questions afresh. Earlier, these questions were taken as finally resolved and without much controversy. Things were 'taken for granted'. But the new developments rapidly contradicted the established notions. Natural sciences in 19th-20th centuries caused an upheaval in the established classical concepts. Physics in particular forced a re-evaluation of philosophical concepts, a reworking and fresh discussion. It goes to the credit of physics and its new discoveries that worldview and philosophy once again came to the centre of attention and discussion. Philosophy and physics, as also the natural sciences in general, have become inseparable in the 20th and 21st centuries, with every discovery forcing a philosophical discussion.

From Tangible Objects to 'Field'

The tangible world is a small part of reality. Lighted world is only four percent of the reality, and out of that only a small part is known to us. It is only now that we are entering into the world where tangible objects are absent.

Electromagnetism caused the first major cracks in the well-ordered 'Newtonian' image of the world of material objects. It was found that the field existed as an *independent entity* in its own right. It was qualitatively new kind of entity and a step away from *mechanistic world image and its mechanistic description*. In the 18th century, the concept of density and velocity fields were used in hydrodynamics. They dealt with the properties of the molecules constituting the field. This point of view was applied by Faraday, Maxwell and other scientists into the electrodynamics.[20] The *concept of field* constituted an enrichment of the conceptual basis of physics in particular and *philosophy in general*. In addition to the motion of bodies through the space, the *space itself was now found to be in motion,* with concentrations of fields at certain points in the space with their changing amplitudes. How do cognize field and space in motion while at the same time that we cognize tangible material in space, moving or stationary.

This was *an absolutely new reality*: motion of bodies through the space and the *motion of space itself* constitute qualitatively different realities. Consequently they cause differing views of the world. In the former, we observe motion, in the latter we are with the motion. Moving spaces, that too at high speeds, create our consciousness differently, creating tensions and contradictions of view and thought, giving rise to new epistemological problems. How do we reflect moving spaces? What is our relationship with them at high speeds?

Further, in the quantum electrodynamics, the concept of field has further advantages, with the particle understood in terms of quantized states of field.[21]

At the same time, many scientists continued to stick to the mechanical interpretation and tried to fit in the fields within a mechanistic notion of world. It was enough for them to reduce the reality to fields alone or to the tangible bodies and fields. The field is a continuous being, and therefore is 'non-countable'. This approach also reduces everything in the universe to certain basic quantitative characteristics, which, again, are unchanging. Thus mechanism tries to survive by adjusting the new developments within its fixed concepts.

Reductionism helps mechanism to survive.

Along with the field theory and theory of light, the molecular theory and kinetic theory of gases also undermined the mechanistic philosophy during the 18th and the 19th centuries. Theory of heat postulated that heat is a form of chaotic molecular motion. From it developed the molecular theory of gases. A gas consisted of irregular or chaotic motion of molecules. The molecules moved through the space freely, except when colliding with each other or with the walls.

A strong example of the random molecular motion came from the Brownian motion. The botanist Brown discovered in 1824 that spore particles suspended in water display irregular and perpetual motion without any source of energy. It was shown that this was due to the chaotic molecular motion. Later it was shown that the atoms too move with irregular motion.

The kinetic theory of gases showed that the large-scale statistical regularities are largely independent of the complicated and irregular motions at the micro and atomic levels.

In any given region the effect of the change in a molecule will be countered or averaged out by the numerous other "opposite changes" in the motions of the neighboring molecules.[22] Suppose there is a system or a box of molecules to the order of 10^{23}; behavior of each is impossible to determine, which is all the time undergoing changes. But the same system may well make it possible to predict the overall average and general overall macroscopic average properties of the system without the need for precise information about the individual molecules.[23] Macroscopic average quantities are *insensitive* to the motions and arrangement of the individual molecules.[24]

"Because these mean values depend almost entirely only on the general over-all properties of the molecules, such as the mean density, the mean kinetic energy, etc, *which can be defined directly at the large-scale level,* it becomes possible to obtain regular and predictable relationships *involving the large-scale level alone.*"[25] The macroscopic level possesses relatively *autonomous qualities constituting macroscopic causal laws.*[26]

Following Bohm, the example of water can be taken. It has a set of macroscopic qualities, such as liquidity, wetness, flow, etc. It satisfies certain hydrodynamic relations such as pressure, temperature, density, etc. Therefore, in the consideration of water, we do not treat it as an aggregate of molecules.

According to David Bohm, "The concept of relatively autonomous levels has been found to have rather wide range of application."[27] Beneath the atomic level, there is one of sub-atomic particles or elementary particles, such as electrons, protons, neutrons, etc. There are other levels even below this one.

Electron and Concept of 'Vacuum'

The discovery of electron in 1897 was a major event for physics, science and philosophy. Removal of an electron from a negative-energy state would result in a 'hole' in the vacuum, behaving like a particle of an opposite change, as per Paul Dirac[28]. This was later termed positron, one of the most spectacular discoveries of theoretical physics.[29]

This has led to a radical reorientation of the concept of vacuum itself. In the pre-quantum concept, it was an empty space containing nothing. In the post-classical era, the view tells us that even the vacuum is 'full', whose study requires use of radiation. That means electromagnetism is everywhere. The vacuum is full of activity, it only being at the lowest state of energy. They gave rise to the concept of 'virtual particles', which in fact are active vacuum. This has changed the view and structure of the world radically.[30]

When two electric particles come under the influence of their electromagnetic fields and forces, the disturbance caused mutually is transmitted in form of photons. *This is quite different from the forces between the gravitating bodies like the sun and the earth.* Photons are like rays of particles which behave like wave or particle as required.[31]

This observation is representative of *a world where conversions and motions are the rule.* There is no time to actually 'observe' them. Their motions cannot be stilled and observed, cannot be seen and measured at leisure. The motions have to be derived and calculated. There are no stable objects; the 'objects' in fact are waves and particles at constant speeds, which are all the time 'not there', a world constructed by and composed of energy transformations. Our tools of knowledge undergo a change, taking us into a reality where nothing is stable. Our worldview must change so as to grasp this reality.

It is "much more natural to regard the particles as different states of excitement of matter."[32] It is a reorientation of the classical picture of matter, in particular of the particle. The very concept of particle has to change. Matter lies more between the 'heavenly', tangible bodies in a continuous state of excitement, moving at the speed of light or near-about.

Conceptual Structure of Mechanistic Philosophy

Developments in 18th and 19th centuries enriched conceptual structure of physics and philosophy. They included the concept of levels, qualitative changes leading to quantitative changes, mean behavior of large bodies, etc. Though not in contradiction, they represent a step away from mechanism. They contradict the idea of absolute and final fundamental laws, quantitative in form.

In the original form of mechanistic philosophy, notions of qualitative change and of chance were considered subjective aids to our thinking on matter, meaning thereby that they did not exist in the material reality. It is an important characteristic of mechanical materialism that it allows limitless number of adjustments in the details of the world picture. Qualitative changes are only shadows of quantitative changes, and only adjustments of the over-all view.

The basic assumption of the mechanistic view was that the

world was made up of atoms with quantitative characteristics, from which everything else followed. It was discovered that the atoms were composed of electrons, protons and neutrons in motion, which broke the picture of world and made it impossible for the laws of atomic motions *alone* to govern the reality. Atoms and the macroscopic realities were in constant inter-reactions. The particles within the atoms created another level of reality.[33]

Let us take the example of *temperature*. According to atomic theory, temperature is completely and perfectly determined by the mean kinetic energy of the atomic and molecular motions. At temperatures of a few thousand degrees, atoms and molecules dissociate into electrons and ions. They have qualitatively different qualities than those of undissociated systems.[34] At temperatures millions of degrees, even nuclei begin to transform. Thus the idea that temperature is the result of the mean kinetic energy of the chaotic atoms and molecules *ceases to exist*.

Within the classical framework, the concept of 'rise in temperature' is directly related with the motions and displacement of atoms and molecules through space. This concept confirms the motion through space, during which time, atoms are kept intact, they exist in their 'being'. They contribute to the definition of the 'atom' even while being autonomous and in motion. While the molecules and atoms may separate from each other quantitatively, changing the nature and motion of the 'things' they constitute, *they themselves remain largely unaffected*. They continue to constitute the world! The "...original mechanistic assumption that this determination is not approximate and conditional, but instead perfect and absolute"[35] continues to operate. The laws and concepts of the macroscopic world are sought to be applied to the atom. This approach leads to *a serious conflict in the world-view*.

Further developments show that the atom is divided

into electrons, protons and neutrons. They begin to display *independence from the classical laws* that constitute the atom, and from the motions related with particular temperatures. They acquire their own motions or become free to display their own dialectics. These particles also get transformed into qualitatively different kinds of particles in high energy collisions with each other. This is different from collisions between tangible bodies. In temperatures beyond a certain range, laws of atomic levels become inapplicable. Since atoms are not the fundamental units nor are even the electrons etc, the universal nature of the classical laws collapses.

For example, the gamma rays burst are the most energetic and luminous *electromagnetic* event. It can release more energy in ten seconds than our sun will emit in its entire ten billion year life! This is an example of total breakdown of the classical, atomic and sub-atomic laws. How do we explain this reality?! It is a multi-billion history compressed in ten seconds! And to unravel the ten seconds, we need to travel ten billion years!! *This is the crisis of cognition.* Cognition must raise itself anew on an entirely different basis.

The serious limitations of the philosophy of the mechanical age including materialism get exposed. The base of philosophy is changed and shifts to rapid motions. The philosophy has to philosophize more about speeds and conversion that about the material realities. It is the motion which is the object of philosophy not the thing or matter. The deeper one goes, the greater the inadequacies of existing philosophy are exposed.

There is an interesting relation between qualitative and quantitative aspects of the transition *out of* the mechanical state. The precise form of forces between molecules, defining their laws of motion depends upon the qualitative state of matter such as gas, liquid or solid. Here the motions and relations of atoms and molecules are affected, but not the electrons, protons and neutrons constituting the atoms. There are stars in which there are no atoms but there certainly dense clouds of electrons etc.[36] Behavior of electrons etc may be quite different than when they are inside the atoms.

Bohm makes an interesting formulation that "every mechanical law applies only to an isolated system".[37] This is because the behavior of the isolated system depends on its boundary conditions. That leads to the creation of independent systems *external* to one another. That means mechanistic approach loses meaning when the *system becomes continuous*. What is external becomes *internal*, the inner dialectics of the new system. Electromagnetism and quantum mechanics are good examples of this radical qualitative transformation. Preciseness at macro level leads to that at micro levels, with mechanics progressively losing its relevance.

The system increasingly loses its relevance as a relation between two or more bodies, and becomes a relation between motions and fleeting, momentary creations, popping up and out of concentrations of matter and energy. Quality more and more is converted into quantitative expressions with their own quantities. In history of thought and observation, quality of object has played the decisive role. Quantities have been subordinated to such observations.

Situation is now reversed. Qualities must now dissociate themselves into quantities, which in turn display absolutely different kinds of qualities, with approximations to reality. This is an important source of neo-positivism, transcendentalism and subjective objectivism. Mathematical points and statistical motions convert or reduce objects into mere quantities, *leading to a loss of experience*. This 'loss of experience' is a *new experience* for humanity, and consequently for human thought. This diversion in philosophy needs serious adjustment in terms of new realities, or 'realities' as produced by our interaction with sub-atomic and quantum levels.

Thought and contemplation at light speed is quite a different proposition, *a qualitative break with the past*. They cannot be explained by our falling back into the past modes of thinking; new modes have to be evolved.

Thought has to adjust with growing speeds of material forms, transitional forms, and leading up to light speed, an unprecedented event in the history of thought. Thought so far has been a product of ordinary and natural material speeds and motions. It has emerged and evolved in the course of these speeds. In fact thought and consciousness have emerged due to 'slowdown' of speeds with the formation of the planet earth. At high speeds, thought is not the 'reflection of reality' in the consciousness; rather it is the unity and identity of the brain and consciousness with brain-like and consciousness-like reality. They constitute one single continuous reality.

The laws of the quantum domain are basically quantitative in nature. These quantities basically express *new qualities*, which are exceedingly fleeting, and can only be expressed in so many calculations necessary to cover the various aspects of motions. They are expressed in certain probabilities, which ultimately constitute the tangible reality. For example, in the post-classical worldview, a particle is not really a particle but the probability of being a particle, which at the same time is also wave or waves. Probability is the determinant factor of determinism. What we see at the tangible level we do not, cannot, 'see' at probabilistic levels, where we derive reality from *our interaction with the unknown reality*. We begin by assuming that what we interact with is reality we delved into, but it reveals itself as so many quantitative figures representing motions of higher orders. High motions convert our observations into quantities about transformations, which can only be expressed *as quantities*. Yet these quantities are the onset of qualitatively new reality, which reveals itself in and through new qualities. Our consciousness finds itself face to face with new processes of formation of structures of consciousness.

We had so far thought that the world consisted of, was made up of, 'things', objects and processes related with them.

It was enough to make an orderly study of the objects existing outside our consciousness, to study their reflection on our brain, and we 'understood' the world or the reality *out there*. Epistemology ended there, except in the quantitative sense. The world consisted of various types of objects of shapes and sizes, with empty spaces in between, and these objects moved *in time and space*. They were reflected in our brains producing corresponding ideas.

But now the object of our study is unstable, and though existing outside our consciousness, they hardly 'exist' in the older sense. They do not exist in time and space. We are therefore left without them, rudderless. It is difficult for us to think without recourse to time and space. The objective reality is on the move constantly, moving 'unrealistically', making it almost impossible to catch it. *Therefore our study concerns more with motions than with objects*. They do not produce fixed images in our brain; the images are constantly changing. We move relative to the surrounding world of objects and their movement or non-movement, but in the non-Cartesian world, *we have no reference point*, and it becomes difficult to establish our relation with this world, which seemingly does not have a reference point. We are surrounded by rapid energy conversions and transitions.

The processes existing outside our consciousness are nearer to our brain processes, to the processes of the consciousness. Therefore, there every possibility of consciousness processes and wave/particle dualities affecting each other directly.

The fixed and stationary picture was broken by the discovery of the *electromagnetic field*. For the first time, an 'object' or a reality was discovered which did not fit in with our observations of natural objects, whether on the earth or out in the space. Now we are confronted with the 'unnatural' objects, that is, not naturally occurring. It was found that electromagnetism filled the empty spaces between the tangible objects, which so far were considered to be active due to the 'action at a distance', that is *through* the 'empty' spaces. Now the space was not empty but full of high-energy matter, and of qualitatively different kind.

In brief, electromagnetism creates a field of waves and particles, which convey forces, energy, and signals across the field. They connect the tangible objects with each through the exchange of waves, particles and energy. So this causes a fundamental shift in our worldview. We need to modify our picture with the addition of objects which we must grasp in their high motion. This grasping is not direct, and involves not only advanced equipments, experiments and calculations but also a new worldview. A relation has to be established now between the new discoveries and the existing realities. The process of 'observation' goes deeper and the nature of it changes.

What is the world of electromagnetism like? It is a world of waves, particles, wave-lengths, frequencies, and such other realities. And they all operate at light speed or near light speed. How to connect with such speeds and motions? What and how is our relation with them? How do we philosophize about them?

There is motion in the Newtonian world, but it is fixed and orderly, and therefore our thoughts too are orderly. The motion in the new world is exceedingly rapid, and our study is more of the motion than of the object. These two are qualitatively different kinds of motion, leading to different kinds of world reality.

NOTES

1. See, James Gillies, *CERN and the Higgs Boson*, Icon, London, 2018, pp. 12-13.
2. Bertrand Russell, *History of Western Philosophy*, George Allen and Unwin Ltd, London, 1947, p. 85.
3. Ibid.
4. Ibid, p. 92.
5. Ibid, p. 269.

6. Marx and Engels, *Collected Works*, Vol. 1, Moscow, p. 34.
7. Ibid, p. 48, emphasis in the original.
8. Samuel Enoch Stumpf, *Socrates to Sartre: A History of Philosophy*, McGraw-Hill, 1982, p. 290.
9. Ibid.
10. Albert Einstein, *Ideas and Opinions*, Rupa Publications, 2019, p. 253.
11. Ibid, p. 254.
12. Ibid.
13. Ibid, pp. 254-55.
14. David Bohm, *Causality and Chance in Modern Physics*, Routledge, London, 1984, pp. 34-35.
15. Ibid, p. 35, emphasis added.
16. Ibid, p. 38.
17. Ibid.
18. Ibid.
19. Ibid.
20. Ibid, p. 45.
21. Ibid, Footnote, pp. 45-46.
22. Ibid, p. 50.
23. Ibid.
24. Ibid.
25. Ibid, p. 50, emphasis in the original.
26. Ibid.
27. Ibid, p. 51.
28. See, Jagjit Singh, *Space and Time Waltz*, Publications and Information Directorate, and Wiley Eastern Limited, 1995, p. 80.
29. Ibid, p. 81.
30. Ibid.
31. Ibid, pp. 83-84.
32. Ibid, p. 93.
33. Ibid, pp. 57-58.
34. Ibid, p. 58.
35. Ibid.
36. Ibid, p. 60.
37. Ibid, p. 61.

2

Electromagnetism and Field: Reality at Light Speed

With electromagnetism we enter the world of high speeds of up to light speeds, the world of unimaginable qualities and extra-ordinary quantities. This reality is constituted of a wide range of waves and wave-lengths, and momentary particles. It is unlike anything we had in our history. It is exact opposite of the world we witnessed so far. It fills the spaces between the tangible objects. Time becomes the determining factor in this world: 'reality' is fashioned according to higher speeds. In other words time is the determining factor.

What is reality at light speed? This is the new question we have now to tackle. We have to begin our philosophical investigations afresh.

Light and other forms of electromagnetic radiation consist of precise frequencies, wavelengths and measurements of qualitatively different kind. Red light has a relatively long wavelength, blue has relatively short. For the visible light, it is about 5 ten-thousands of a millimeter. As traffic lights change from red through yellow to green, the wavelength decreases from 7.0 to 5.8 to 5.3 ten thousands of an mm.

Frequency is the rushing of the waves past a point. Frequency for visible light is 600 trillion cycles per second ($6x10^{14}$ cycles/sec or 6×10^{14} hertz or Hz). Red light has low frequency of about 440 trillion cycles per second, while blue light has a relatively high frequency of 640 trillion cycles/sec.

The reality consists of a wide range of wavelengths from high frequencies and short wavelengths to low frequencies and long wavelengths. They include gamma rays, x-rays, colors of the visible light like 'vibgyor'.[1] *Visible light is only a small part of reality.* Visible world constitutes a very small proportion, only 4 per cent, of the existing reality. We know nothing about the non-visible world; we know very little about the visible world. The base of our consciousness is very narrow and exceedingly limited.

Blows to Newtonian Picture of World: Field and Electromagnetism

Field theory was one of the major transitions to the micro-levels of reality. It shook the existing notions of the world. Newton's theory of motion received another major blow from Maxwell's theory of electromagnetism. "It became clear that the electric and magnetic interactions between bodies were effected, not by forces operating instantaneously at a distance, but by processes which are propagated through space at a finite speed."[2]

Thus qualitatively new forces and new realities emerged, which by their speed and time determinations created *new realities*.

Field

In 19th century a new type of causal factors and laws appeared, those related with the field. It was felt by the end of 19th century that the laws of electricity and magnetism could not be satisfactorily explained within the framework of the Newtonian laws. Therefore the entities of electric and magnetic *fields* were added. In the Newtonian scheme of world, the bodies were localized in a definite space and moved with a definite speed, in definite time. Contrary to this, the fields were spread out in a continuous distribution in the space. At particular point in space and at particular instant of time, the fields: have definite values. Force would be exerted on a unit electric point and unit magnetic pole. Knowledge of the position and velocities in a given system helped to determine the position and velocities of all other bodies.[3]

Electric charges in motion create magnetism and magnetism in motion creates electric field. Fields change in value at each instant of motion. Fields and bodies co-determine each other. Complete causal laws include both bodies and fields. Waves are produced in which electric and magnetic fields oscillate. The predicted velocity of the electromagnetic waves was equal to that of light. Thus arose the electromagnetic theory of light. A wide range of fields was covered including x-rays, gamma rays, infra red to ultra-violet, etc.[4]

"The introduction of the fields evidently involves a fundamental modification of our concept of matter and of space."[5] The fields carry energy, momentum, etc simulating the properties of moving bodies. According to Einstein, fundamental particles of physics like electrons, protons etc may carry pulse like concentrations of moving field. So they are particular *modes of motion* of the fields. Thus many of the properties of the material bodies (system) are shown to be dependent on the fields. The *concept of matter* thus is expanded to include the expanding and moving fields.[6] They expand through, in and as space, as representing certain manifestations of the material system. In addition to the motion of bodies through space, qualitatively new kinds of motion were discovered involving a set of changing amplitudes of fields at various points of space.[7]

The hypothesis of existence of field in its own right was *"an important step away from 'mechanism'"*.[8]

Initially, the 'field' passes through the phase wherein one has to fill in the space between the material bodies. Therefore, we imagine them to be an 'extension' of the material bodies. But as we move further in our investigations, we discover new realities, which are not an extension of and subservient to the tangible reality, but a reality independent in itself, and a reality qualitatively different from the one existing. In fact, we begin to stumble upon the fact that tangibles themselves are the product of the high speed realities through *a slowdown of time*. Without such a slowdown, the tangibles like the earth cannot come into being.

Electromagnetism involves study of electromagnetic field consisting of interaction between electrically charged particles. Electromagnetic force is carried by fields composed of electric and magnetic fields, together giving rise to the 'electromagnetic field'. They are responsible for electromagnetic radiation, such as the visible light and invisible range of waves.

Originally, electricity and magnetism were considered separate phenomena. But James Clerk Maxwell in his *A Treatise on Electricity and Magnetism* in 1873 showed that they constitute a single unified phenomenon. The field is made up of different waves and wave-lengths, moving at the speed of light. These waves constitute *a field*.

It is difficult to reconcile electromagnetism with classical mechanics. Classical mechanics is the study of the motion of the macroscopic bodies. Motion of the machines and its parts, projectiles, trains, ships, other vehicles, rockets, spacecraft, planets, stars, rocks, stones, rivers, etc and their motions are covered by the classical mechanics.

The first scientist to pose a challenge to the Newtonian scenario was the English experimental scientist Michael Faraday (1791-1861). His and Maxwell's discoveries led to the development of the concept of the 'field', which was a major theoretical, practical and philosophical breakthrough. There is a magnetic field, and there is an electric field. In the course of time it was found that they constituted a single whole of the electromagnetic field. A common experience will help us get an idea of the 'field'. If iron filings are placed on a piece of paper and a magnet put under it, the filings get organized into 'magnetic lines of force'. They thus point to the existence of a magnetic field. Similarly, an electrically charged body creates an electric field.

These fields *oscillate* and move along in the 'space'. An oscillating magnetic field gives rise to an oscillating electric field and *vice versa*. According to Maxwell's equations, electric and magnetic fields push each other through the empty space *at the speed of light*. Maxwell showed that when the fields propagated, as electromagnetic waves, they carried definite amounts of energy. Thus energy could be transported from place to place. This was confirmed by Hertz. Radio waves actually carry energy.[9]

Electromagnetism is a force which holds together the matter that forms solid bodies, holds together atoms in molecules, and electrons in atoms. That is how the living beings and the chemical reactions and chemical bodies exist. Electromagnetism operates in the neurons of our brain. It governs processing of information. It creates friction, turns electric motor and combustion engine, turn on lights and help us listen radio.

An understanding of this force involves crucial modification to the world of Newton, leading to the modern physics. *This is the notion of field.*[10]

Faraday intuited something new in the existing picture: "we must not think of forces acting directly between distant objects, as Newton presumed. We must instead think that there exists an entity diffused throughout space, which is modified by electric and magnetic bodies."[11] Faraday sees the field as bundles formed of infinitely thin 'lines of force' filling everything around us. They carry force and transmit electricity and magnetism. Through them two objects with electrical charges interact. The forces of the two objects are 'carried' by field's lines. Two distant charged objects do not attract or repel each other directly *but through the field in between them.*

Newton too had doubts: he suspected that something existed between two objects, but he was not clear, and left the question "to the consideration of my Readers."![12]

By implication, Maxwell explains what light is. "Maxwell realizes that his equations predict that Faraday's lines can tremble and undulate..."[13] He computed the speed of Faraday's lines and found them to be same as that of light. Maxwell understood that light is nothing but *trembling* of Faraday's lines. It was a great transition from the tangible bodies and their laws of motion to the discovery of the intangible matter, wherein these laws proved inoperable.

We see the world around us. How do we see it? Between various objects, there is the sea of the vibrating waves moving at light speed, which transport their images to us. We also see the world in different colors, which identify different objects. "We see the world around us in color. What is color?" Put simply, it is the *frequency* (speed of oscillation) *of the electromagnetic waves* that light is.[14] The receptors of our eyes distinguish between electromagnetic waves of different frequencies, giving rise to different colors. What we see are the *vibrating* Faraday lines! A world is explained at last, a world that was mysterious so far. So, the discovery of electromagnetism was a revolution in the in the way we viewed colors and the world itself. The revolution had only begun.

It is for the first time that what we see and how is explained. It is the electromagnetic waves that affect our eyes and brain, but we thought we 'saw' the things and objects themselves and their motions. There was discovered something that connected our observation with object. The process was completed or is the beginning of 'completion'.

Color is the speed of the vibration of Faraday's lines. The vibrations are determined by the electric charges emitting light. The charges are the electrons moving within the atom.[15] Electromagnetic waves are not only vibrations of Faraday's lines but also swarms of photons. Photons are the *quanta* of the electromagnetic field.[16] With the discovery of the quantum, the dividing line between field and particle disappears. Particles are quanta of a field.[17]

Paul Dirac simplifies the description of nature by discovering a convergence between the notion of particle as used by Newton and the notion of field used by Faraday.[18] Not only are the particles diffused in space like fields but the fields interact like particles. The notions of fields and particles merge together in quantum mechanics.[19] They were separate in Faraday and Maxwell. "The *cloud of probability* which accompanies electrons between one interaction and another does resemble a field."[20]

The *energy* of Faraday's lines (electromagnetic field) can take on only certain values, and not others. Consequently the field behaves like a set of packets of energy. These are the quanta of energy discovered by Planck.[21] "Particles are quanta of a field, just as photons are quanta of light. All fields display a granular structure in their interactions."[22]

Thus the field of electromagnetism is not only a continuous existence, it also has a *granular* character.

The following are some peculiar features of 'field'. The electromagnetic field consists, among others, of electrons, photons and field quanta. Electron has itself has its own field. Here we make a transition. The waves *appear* as particles after interaction. The electron or the quantum of the field or the photon do not follow a trajectory in space, but appear at a given place when interacting. There is a transformation in particle. We do not know when and where the particle/s will appear. This is a different kind of particle, a break with our past understanding of particle, the classical particle.[23]

One has to reach the conclusion that the field and the particle are the same thing! "The notions of fields and the particles, separated by Faraday and Maxwell, end up merging in quantum mechanics."[24] It is the photons that interact with our eyes, and not the fields or the waves.

Faraday's lines also vibrate at lower frequencies, more slowly than light, giving rise to other waves produced by electric motion, not seen by our eyes. All modern communication is the application of Faraday lines and Maxwell equations, leading to telephone, radio, satellite, computer, internet, etc types of communication. The current communication technology is based on the use of electromagnetic waves, a *revolutionary discovery.*

But here arose a problem which created ripples and crises in the established thought and worldview. The problem is that *electromagnetism moves with the speed of light!* How to relate a thing moving with earthly speed with something moving at light speed?! This is a practical, theoretical as well as a philosophical question. It is an *epistemological* question as well.

Electromagnetism moves with magnetic and electric force alternatively at light speed. We will not, need not, go into technical details but only state that electromagnetism consists of waves of different but precise wave-lengths and frequencies. Among the implications of Maxwell's equations was that electric and magnetic fields would 'push' each other through empty space. An oscillating magnetic field gives rise to an oscillating electric field, which in turn would cause an oscillating magnetic field, and so on. All this happens at the speed of light![25]

In 1905, Einstein showed that light waves are different from say water waves. In contrast to water waves, light waves keep themselves going only by virtue of one part going forward and powering up the next part.

In the late 1850s, Maxwell extended the Faraday's idea of 1821 of electricity and magnetism, united them and tried to 'see' what was happening *inside a light beam*. The electricity part shimmers forward, squeezing out a magnetic part; then the magnetic part creates a further 'surge' of electricity, repeating the rushing cycle. *Whenever one thought being close to a wave, it powers out a new one hurtling away from you and ahead.* Light is always *hurtling away* from us.[26]

When a light beam starts going forward, a little bit of electricity is produced, and as it moves forward, it produces magnetism, which then produces electricity, and so on. Maxwell termed these fast jumps as 'mutual embrace'. So light is nothing but a series of these leapfrogging jumps.[27]

"Light will always be a quick leapfrogging of electricity out from magnetism, and then of magnetism leaping out from electricity. All swiftly shooting away..."[28]

Comparison of flow of water through pipes etc to the 'flow' of electromagnetism is not applicable. The two are qualitatively different. Water flows through the pipe, using the friction of the metal or other solid surface. It consists of molecules of two elements, hydrogen and oxygen, consisting of different numbers of atoms, and it is in a liquid state. The flow of water is mechanical and slow.

It is quite different with the electromagnetic 'flow'. It flows through nothing and moves at light speed. It consists of a wide range of waves and wave lengths. It travels *creating its own waves*. Laws of relativity are essential to understand its motion. The area around the electromagnetic event is filled with 'field', a complex of exceedingly fast motions of waves and particles. The world of flows changes dramatically, and so must also our approach and outlook.

It is a world of charged particles in motion, with field as an area of influence of force.[29] Electrical force acts between the charged particles and the magnetic force between charged particles in motion. Consequently, light (electromagnetism) is a 'field in flight'.[30]

Einstein developed the concept of photon in 1905. Photon is a packet of *electromagnetic energy*. It was named by the American chemist GN Lewis in 1916. It is a messenger particle carrying a force between the originating and the receiving particles, such as electrons, nucleus, etc. "The photon is the messenger particle for the electromagnetic field, carrying the force between the interacting particles and travelling at the speed of light.[31]

This is light or electromagnetism, only able to exist when

moving forward, at the particular speed. Faraday and Maxwell wondered how did it move forward. This insight was lurking in the Maxwell's equations.[32] They were solved by Einstein in the above-mentioned manner.

That means in order just to *exist,* light must keep on moving at a particular speed. This is an amazing reality, and is among the greatest mysteries, and is an example of *dialectics of nature* at work, where *motion is the basis of the very existence.*

In the mechanical world too, the object has motion. It moves through space. It changes. To trace the source of motion in the mechanical world, one has to use dialectical method extensively to uncover each step of motion. But in the post-classical world, the object dissociates to produce motions without tangibility.

Introduction of the concept of field involves a fundamental modification of the concepts of matter and space.[33] The concept implies that even when there are no 'bodies', there existed a different world made of varying fields. It is world without bodies, materials and direct observations. They carry momentum, angular momentum, energy etc, and display some characteristics of bodies in motion. "Thus the concept of matter has effectively been expanded to include the notion of field...", which spreads through broad regions of space.[34]

One of the assumptions of the classical (Newtonian) mechanics was that the properties of matter are continuously variable.[35] This notion breaks down at the atomic scale, forcing evolution of a new system of mechanics, the quantum mechanics. It was known from Maxwell's electromagnetic theory that charged particles moving around curved paths radiated electromagnetic radiation (energy). In Newton and Maxwell, this should go on continuously, with the orbiting electron losing energy and spiraling into the nucleus. Thus the classical theory of Newton and the discovery by Maxwell, both had the 'collapse of the atom' in-built into them. The quantum theory predicted discrete non-radiating energy levels in which the wave associated with the electron just fitted around the nucleus. This formed standing wave patterns.[36]

Electromagnetism is *both an abstract construct and a reality.* It all depends on the *stage of development of science.* David Deutsch was asked whether the electromagnetism is really 'out there' or just an abstract concept. He answered that it is both, that "It is certainly an abstract construct, but it gains its place in physics when a physical theory says that it corresponds to something real. What words we then attach to this real thing that it corresponds to, is a subsidiary matter."[37]

The laws of classical mechanism break down at this speed and are not applicable. We stumble upon a different kind of reality. The determining or main feature of the new reality is high speeds of the events/processes. At this motion, atoms and other objects will not be stable and will be converted into waves. It is not possible for matter to remain intact at this speed; they get converted into energy. As will be seen, these waves themselves will give rise to new problems, unleashing new structures of reality and its motion, including that of quantum. Our *historically constructed notion of particle dissolves on meeting this reality.*

This was the first major development, which shook the concepts of the classical world.

Classical Atomism and Electromagnetism as Opposite Poles of Cognition

Thus the Newtonian world is *negated* by the discovery of field and electromagnetism, which are *exact opposite* of the former in every sense. The tangibility is lost, motions are instant, the mechanical laws collapse, and matter is constituted in most intangible continuous form as motion of energy, rather of the processes we cannot catch hold of: this is movement at the speed of light, quite a different matter altogether! Stability and tangibility disappear, and we cannot talk of limited matter which we can see and form ideas about. Existing philosophy collapses and now has to reinvent itself. *Atom is needed no more* and waves rule the roost. Atom undergoes a basic transformation, and through this change it disappears altogether. The new particles within the atom become free to enjoy independent existence and display their qualities fully! Electron for example is now a 'free' particle.

The concept of particle (atom, electron, etc) in the 19th century was still deeply under the Newtonian influence. According to Richard Feynman, the attempts to understand motion of electron around atom using mechanical laws were a complete failure.[38] Classical theory was under increased pressure due to this and other discoveries.

"In the Newtonian picture of the world", particles are visualized simply as any other tangible body, big and small. They act upon each other, move around, operate at a distance, and rebound off each other.[39] Fixed particles and atoms moved around and constituted forms of realities. These particles were clearly distinguishable, were 'out there' for us to discover, discharged functions, etc. They surrounded us, hit us and other materials and went their ways. They were fixed, their paths fixed, and their action and reaction equal and opposite.

This is what determined both our practical as well as the philosophical approach to the world. Electromagnetism broke through the limitations of the classical atom and brought us on the verge of the world of wave/particle duality.

The position, velocities and masses are physically/mathematically determined, and can be determined every time the measurement is made in the earthly conditions. Can particles too behave similarly and measure similarly?

"The Newtonian billiard ball picture of reality is indeed a *deterministic* model." The physical behavior is determined for all times in past or future.[40]

We can no more carry forward the 'billiard ball' picture of the world. The 'ball' now consists of waves and transitory particles, all the time popping up and out. The ball (particle) appears and disappears as an expression of space (field) and resolves itself into waves extending infinitely. We can never return to the particle a second time, and it dissolves every stable structure.

Forces of electricity and magnetism fall off as the inverse square of distance, and electric charge rather than the mass measures the strength of the force.[41]

The fundamentally new ingredient in our picture of the material reality is that the fields are no more mathematical construction, no more appendages to the Newtonian particles, but are actual carriers of definite amounts of energy. Electromagnetic waves indeed carry energy, as proved experimentally by Hertz. The radio waves can for example carry energy.[42]

The problem with classical interpretation of the world is that they carry two kinds of objects: particles with definite parameters, and fields with infinite number of parameters. All energy flows from the particles into the fields. Due to the phenomenon called equi-partition, energy should get evenly distributed. Particles would be without energy. Motions of particles would be converted into waves.

In the Rutherford model of atom (1911), solar system picture is replicated at atomic level. The place of planets is taken by electrons, and of the sun by the nucleus. The particles of the atom are held by electromagnetism rather than by gravitation. According to the classical theory, the orbiting electrons should emit electromagnetic waves of intensity rising very rapidly to infinity, in a tiny fraction of a second. The electrons must plunge into the nucleus![43]

But that does not happen. What happens actually is quite inexplicable on the basis of classical theory.[44] Atoms emit electromagnetic waves but only in bursts of specific discreet frequencies.[45]

Field is the motion of waves and particles, moving at near light speeds. The particle no more acts and interacts *in a leisurely mechanical manner*, creating elements, molecules, compounds and so on. It has no time for step by step reactions, and for creation of subjective ideas.

But the new reality is motion personified. It is composed of motion only.

NOTES

1. Based on Peter Atkins, *Galileo's Finger: The Ten Great Ideas of Science*, Oxford University Press, 2003, pp. 202-03.
2. Albert Einstein, *Ideas and Opinions*, Rupa Publications, 2019, p. 259.
3. Based on David Bohm, *Causality and Chance in Modern Physics*, Routledge, London, 1984, p. 43.
4. Ibid, pp. 43-44.
5. Ibid, p. 45.
6. Ibid, pp. 45-46.
7. Ibid, See Ibid, p. 45.
8. Ibid, p. 45, emphasis added.
9. See, Roger Penrose, *The Emperor's New Mind*, Oxford University Press, 1999, pp. 242-43.
10. Carlo Rovelli, *Reality is Not What It Seems: A Journey to Quantum Gravity*, Penguin Books, 2017, p. 39.
11. Ibid, p. 41.
12. Ibid, p. 43.
13. Ibid, p. 45.
14. Ibid.
15. See, ibid, p. 97.
16. Ibid, p. 108.
17. Ibid.
18. Ibid, p. 107.
19. Ibid.
20. Ibid, p. 107, emphasis added.
21. Ibid.
22. Ibid, p. 108.
23. See, ibid, p. 112.
24. Ibid, p. 107.

25. Roger Penrose, *The Emperor's New Mind*, p. 240-41.
26. David Bodanis, *E=MC²: A Biography of the World's Most Famous Equation*, Pan Books, London, 2000, p. 49.
27. Ibid, p. 47.
28. Ibid, p. 50.
29. Peter Atkins, *Galileo's Finger... etc*, p. 180.
30. Ibid.
31. Ibid, p. 181.
32. Ibid, pp. 49, 48.
33. David Bohm, *Causality and Chance...etc*, p. 44.
34. Ibid, p. 45.
35. Davies and Brown, *The Ghost in the Atom*, Cambridge University Press, Canto Edition, p. 1.
36. Ibid, p. 3.
37. Ibid, p. 94.
38. Richard P. Feynman, *QED: The Strange Theory of Light and Matter*, Universities Press, 1999, p. 5.
39. See, Penrose, *The Emperor...etc*, p. 238.
40. Ibid, p. 219.
41. Ibid, pp. 238-39.
42. Ibid, pp. 242-43.
43. Ibid, p. 295.
44. Ibid.
45. Ibid.

3

Classical to Post-classical Reality: A Critique of Mechanistic and Idealistic Views by Einstein

In his "Autobiographical Notes"[1], Albert Einstein presents a detailed critique of mechanism or mechanistic world outlook, and shows how electromagnetism and wave-optics penetrated and destroyed it.

Einstein while dealing with these questions first defines 'thinking' as not a simple perception or reflection but as a process formation of concepts. "What precisely is 'thinking'? When, at the reception of sense-impressions, memory-pictures emerge, this is not yet 'thinking'. And when such pictures form series... this too is not yet 'thinking'. When however a certain picture turns up in many such series, then...it becomes an ordering element for such series... Such an element becomes an instrument, a concept. I think that the transition from free association or 'dreaming' to thinking is characterized by the dominating role which the 'concept' plays in it. It is by no means necessary that a concept must be connected with a sensorily cognizable and reproducible sign (word)..."[2]

This presentation is crucial to our discussion, though not without objections and amendments. Thinking is solely human characteristic, not found in animals. Thinking goes through many stages in human brain, including reflection, perceptions, generalization and memory. Perception is a little farther/deeper than mere reflection. Human thought goes deeper from simple reflection to perception to concepts. Without perception and impressions, there can be no thinking and thoughts. Einstein is right in stating that formation of concept is crucial to thinking, but this is a crucial stage in thought-formation. Besides, memory picture is an advanced stage of thought because it presumes certain formation of structure of thought.

With the penetration of thought into the sub-atomic domains, it enters qualitatively different levels, both subjective and objective. This is a *crucial transition* being made by human thought.

Einstein refers to the *History of Mechanics* by Ernst Mach, which influenced him greatly. Though initially impressed, Einstein later considered Mach's position as untenable. Einstein criticizes him for not placing "in the correct light the essentially constructive and speculative nature of thought and more especially of scientific thought; in consequence of which he condemned theory on precisely those points where its constructive-speculative character unconcealably comes to light..."[3]

Mach's philosophical ideas failed to become the basis for Einstein's worldview.[4]

Ernst Mach belonged to the school of positivists and empirio-criticists of the 19th-20th centuries. Avenarius, Bogdanov and some others were its prominent protagonists. This philosophy has been sharply criticized by Lenin in his famous work *Materialism and Empirio-criticism*. This school and that of the 'Vienna Circle' over-emphasize the role of 'experience' in observation and in developing concepts based upon scientific and experimental facts. Sensory experience is detached step by step from the objectively existing material reality, is isolated, and is reduced to the sole thought-making element or factor. He said, in mentally separating a body from environment in which it moves, "what we really do is to extricate a group of sensations on which our thoughts are fastened...from the stream of all our sensations."[5] Mathematical functions were more important to describe the sensory perceptions.[6]

Empirio-criticism is a more rigorous form of positivism which reduced knowledge to our sensations, to pure experience. It was on this basis that he rejected the atomic model and such other concepts/realities, as they could be directly experienced, and criticized the atomic hypothesis of Boltzmann.

Thus, the Machian approach reduced the reality to direct experience alone, totally negating, in effect, the material reality. The scientific analysis of the material reality is one thing, while denying the very existence of it another. These are two separate things. Reductionism ultimately leads to subjective idealism and consequently to a non-scientific approach.

Also, 'experience' can be direct and indirect. The experience at micro-levels is not direct or less and less so as we penetrate deeper. We reach conclusions about them through various scientific assumptions and mathematical calculations, which in themselves are reflections of reality. These realities are certainly of different kind, with no direct contact and experience, such as in quantum science. But they are reality all the same.

Lenin quotes Mach from his *Analysis of Sensations* regarding philosophy thus: "What we call matter is a certain systematic combination of *elements* (sensations)."[7] Mach says, "For us matter is not what is primarily given. Rather, what is primarily given are the elements (which in a certain familiar relation are designated as sensations)..."[8] 'Elements' in Mach are nothing but sensations, as he himself makes clear. Lenin summarizes Mach's idealism[9] and says that it leads to solipsism.[10] Lenin quotes to show that other, many non-materialist philosophers, too criticized Mach for his solipsism.[11]

It is this subjective idealism of logical positivism and solipsism that leads many scientists to empiricism and full acceptance of thought process based on 'experience' alone, which is variously interpreted.

The physicists of 19th century saw in the classical mechanics a firm and final foundation for physics and natural sciences. Consequently, they tried to base Maxwell's electromagnetism in the mechanistic world itself. It was assumed that knowledge of the position and velocities in a given system helped automatically to determine the position and velocities of all other bodies. Even Maxwell and Hertz, who had *by implication* demolished mechanics, in their conscious thinking *adhered* to mechanics as a secure basis for physics.[12]

But then it was found that series of *conversions* have to be effected to translate realities and their reflections in one phase (classical) to another (post-classical). These are conversions and interpretations in transition from one kind of reality to another.

Incorporation of wave-mechanics into the mechanical picture of the world led to the creation of the 'ether', which led a *ghostly existence* alongside the rest of the matter. It was a carry-over of the classical-mechanical view. Ether had to be 'created' at the time as medium of propagation of light. It was imagined to exist because like water and sound, had to be there for light to propagate through. This was a reflection of the widely prevalent *mechanical thinking*.

"The factor which finally succeeded" in forcing scientists give up, after long hesitation, their faith in Newton's mechanics "was the electrodynamics of Faraday and Maxwell".[13] "...this theory and its confirmation by Hertz's experiments showed that there are electromagnetic phenomena which by their very nature are detached from every ponderable matter..." They are the electromagnetic waves in *empty space* consisting of electromagnetic fields.[14] "One got used to operating with these fields as independent substances *without finding it necessary* to give one's self an account of their *mechanical nature*; thus mechanics as the basis of physics was being abandoned almost unnoticeably..."[15]

Since then there exist two types of conceptual elements:

material points with forces at a distance between them; and, *continuous field*. "It presents an intermediate state in physics without a uniform basis for entirety..."[16]

With the passing of time, science increasingly has 'distanced' itself *from what is directly observable*. Things/processes now become *indirectly* observable, giving rise to several philosophical interpretations. The meaning and position of the observer and observation undergo a change. The role of abstraction *increases*. This is a crucial point in the *philosophical transition from the classical to the post-classical*. It needs a re-orientation of our view of things and processes. As Einstein says,[17] the *confrontation* of implications of theory with facts became more difficult and drawn out. After the departure from the mechanical foundations, *method became more important*, to differentiate between the two types of observations.

It is to be noted that the distancing of science from what is directly observable led many philosophers to mysticism, *a priorism*, empiricism, phenomenalism, and in general, to a denial of reality itself. The delving into the depths of matter and material forms, changes in their tangible forms, into the world of high speeds where tangibility and direct observation is lost leads many thinkers astray. It also takes us away from the task of grasping and interpreting the new and deeper world, which is not tangible but real, which may not be real in the older sense but which interacts with our brain processes and establishes a system between brain processes and quantum processes. We go deeper into reality, not away from them through our 'experiences'.

Without a dialectical method, we can't differentiate between the two types of realities. This differentiation largely depends upon our approach to the rapid motions, an analysis of which needs such a dialectical method of analysis.

Maxwell's theory made the transition from forces at a distance to field as the fundamental variable. The incorporation of optics into theory of electromagnetism, with its relation of speed of light to the electric and magnetic system, was the new event with unprecedented possibilities.[18]

Initially electromagnetism was made difficult because electricity and magnetism and their 'fields' were treated as 'elementary variables'. Empty space was treated as a special instance of a dielectric body. *Matter* appeared as the bearer of the field, not space. Thus field could have velocity.[19]

H.A. Lorentz brought about a change in this concept. "In principle a field exists, according to him, only in empty space."[20] Matter, considered as atoms, was the only seat of electric charges, between the material particles was the empty space, *which was the seat of the electromagnetic field*. Particle charges create field, exerting forces upon charges of particles, "thus determining the motion of the latter according to Newton's law of motion." If one compares this with Newton's system, the change is this: action at a distance is replaced by the field.[21]

This was the phase of *dualism*, consisting of the material points and field *side by side*. They were together used as elementary concepts,[22] but simultaneously, they were two different kinds of concepts, at loggerheads with each other.

The revolution begun by the introduction of the field continued further. The quantum revolution of 1900 by Max Planck transformed the nature of particles from material points to quanta, the particles of a different kind.

Einstein concludes that "physics is an attempt conceptually to grasp *reality as it is*, thought independently of its being observed. In this sense one speaks of 'physical reality'... *In Newton's theory reality was determined by a material point in space and time; in Maxwell's theory, by the field in space and time.*"[23]

This statement is equally a philosophical one too. It deals with and explains the nature of matter and its reflection in consciousness. We can as well say that materialist philosophy is an attempt to grasp reality as it is.

Bachelard calls it the "*double philosophy* of the experience of space".[24] 'Double philosophy' consists of the realistic philosophy and the Kantian philosophy. He says this is needed to be replaced by "a *dialectical philosophy* of space, a philosophy at once experimental and rational."[25] According to him, philosophy of *ultra-refined experience* and the philosophy of physical theory are firmly *coupled* in relativity, which is a high point of development of the post-classical theory. New critical philosophy is more subtle and synthetic than the Kantian philosophy was towards the Newtonian science.[26] Bachelard emphasizes the revolutionary nature of profounder dialectical explanation of new and deeper events in science and its relations with philosophy.

In the earlier Newtonian 'arrangement of things', the *unconditioned subject was positioned in absolute space.* While everything around is in mechanical motion, the subject is in relative stability.

In the 'Copernican' revolution brought about by Einstein, both the space and the subject and his/her intuition are *relative. Two absolutes* are destroyed: *one,* now the observer and the observation have no absolute character; *two,* now the extension of the objective world has no absolute character. There is less room for the observer now, the intuition of the observer being relative, the importance of which is enhanced. The result is, as per Einstein, *relativity of the observer.*[27]

These developments take dialectics to deeper, and therefore, to much higher levels.

Where is the 'observer' placed now with the developments in electromagnetism? How do we evaluate him/her and his/her relation with the objective world, which moving at high speed and is in constant transformation? In such a world, the observer never gets an opportunity to pinpoint and fix 'things', which all have become transformed into processes.

As physics transits into electromagnetic stage, less was available for direct experience. The existing meaning of 'experience' is not applicable here. Therefore, the importance of '*a priori*' assumptions and speculative experiences gained ground. But assumptions and calculations cannot be absolutized. Experience is not drawn from experience of the 'external world' anymore. The external world provides us with certain data and details about motions. Such data is more about 'what is not' than about what is. This is because we proceed from our hitherto existing experiences and conclusions. We want to experience, but we come across our relations and reactions with what exists, and then we conclude about what should be or may be existing. The reality before experience is more and more obscured and even clouded.

This is a new factor of the theory of knowledge. How to evaluate what we do not experience at all? This was a crucial problem. How to 'experience' EM waves at 3 lakh km/sec? What does experience mean here? These are crucial philosophical and cognitive questions. This led to the recourse to the categories of Kantian *agnosticism*. A set of scientists transported *a priorism* to reality as a general condition for electromagnetic awareness.

The new notion of *space-time* is indispensable to grasp electromagnetic phenomena. In a Kantian manner, Bachelard says, "one must conceive the *a priori synthesis* which underlies the notion of space-time."[28] He further says that all those who have understood mathematical organization of relativity require no examples like those of passing trains and standing observers.[29] For him *algebraism* and scientific experiment combined synthetically helps grasp Einstein at higher levels. This he designates as the 'rationalistic' revival in Einstein. Here rationalism is interpreted in Kantian sense. Leon Brunschvicg is quoted to this effect: "The advancement on Kant (effected by these new doctrines) consisted in transporting the *a priori* synthesis from the region of intuition to the region of intellect, and this is decisive for the passage to physics."[30]

He fails to explain *apriorism* of space-time.

As per Bachelard, Kantian philosophy holds that space is

not a concept drawn from experience of the external world, since the experience of the space is a *sine qua non* condition of the experience of the external world.[31]

Here we need to be clear that the Kantian interpretation of experience is different from that in science. The Kantian world of experiences is constituted philosophically through the process of abstract cognition. It is a transcendental experience, which traverses the experience of things and acquires philosophical meanings. It will not help in experiences in science or in the absence experience in science. The problem arises when we fail to 'experience' the real world under investigation. Therefore, the Kantian *apriorism* is a shortcut, with fuse, to the explanation of experiences or their absence in the real world; there is a failure of the fuses because of such shortcuts.

Similar is the case with the concept of time. In the same philosophical fashion, "the *space-time algebraic complex* is a *sine qua non* condition of the general validity of our knowledge of electromagnetism."[32]

The knowledge of the electromagnetic phenomena in 19th century was coordinated by the laws of Maxwell. It should be pointed out here that the 19th century concepts were still deeply influenced by Newtonian approach. That meant electromagnetism was still guided by mechanical laws. They must remain invariant even in a change of the reference system. In the course of time, Lorentz transformation formulas emerged because the operation of laws depended upon the frames of reference. The invariance defined the transformation formulas of Lorentz.

These formulas have high philosophical significance for relativity. Lorentz transformations underlie the notion of space-time, forbidding the separation of space and time. Space-time arises of necessity. It is a necessary function of great *philosophical* significance. The role of the philosopher is 'to think thought', and therefore he must think space-time in various aspects of scientific phenomena.[33]

Here the relevance of Kantian *apriorism* breaks down completely. It is shown by the developments of late 19th-early 20th centuries that space and time are *transformed* into space-time due to the new post-classical developments in physics, constantly modified by the frame of reference. Even the measuring rods are constricted. Thus in fact there is no *a priori* space and time; they are the *fresh discoveries* as space-time as a result of discovery of electromagnetism and of quantum and relativity.

Bachelard is unable to come out of the Kantian framework, with its one-sided interpretation of mechanical events dominating 18th century sciences. Space-time is the result of the discovery of electromagnetism itself, and of other discoveries. He unfortunately takes recourse to Kantianism even while discerning rationalism and realism in new physics demanding new philosophy.

Light is an electromagnetic phenomenon, and therefore the notion of space-time is a basic notion for an *ultra-precise* understanding of phenomena.[34] This is a clear contradiction of the Kantian *apriorism,* which is both agnosticism as well as idealism.

EM and Space-time

When light enters the mechanical world, *it renders it precise* in all its aspects. This is a *novel development* in the history of science and philosophy, and also in the world of consciousness. Consciousness and light interact in novel ways. Kantian apriorism and irrationalism in Bachelard tapers down as he deals further on with space-time. At first the concept of space-time is interpreted in an *a priori* fashion, but then it is shown to be installed as functionally primary by *enlightened rationalism,* as space-time constitutes an aspect of relativity. As per Bachelard, there is naïve rationalism in the same sense that there is *naïve realism*. Calculated astronomy provided a 'peace of mind' in contrast to imaginative astronomy.[35] Space-time rids one of the profound reveries of space and time, precludes irrationalism and the mind rests on rationalism.

The 'peace of mind' expression is used here by Bachelard presumably to having achieved a solution of the knotty problems, heaving a sigh of relief.

Achieving 'space-time' through EM and relativity prepares philosophy for philosophical-dialectical inversions and interpenetration of the abstract and the concrete. Space-time is more concrete and realistic despite being a theoretical/intellectual construct.[36] "It is not merely a simple epistemological necessity..."[37] It consolidates and synthesizes two perspectives of experience. Einsteinian science provides a differentiating rationalism, which is *dialectical rationalism*.[38] This is the result of the *philosophical inversion of the abstract and the concrete*.[39] One alternatively proceeds from the concrete to the abstract, and vice versa. Epistemology moves through dialectical opposites, changing their poles.

Classical science and common knowledge have their respective places in epistemology. Dialectics of classical and relativistic mechanics envelopes history of physics. Relativity includes and encompasses all that was known in the 19th century. "Thus relativity permits a retrospective re-enactment of the entire history of mechanistic rationalism."[40]

A profound synthesis between Descartes and Liebniz was achieved by Einstein. The discovery of mathematical-algebraic origin of mass and energy had mathematical rationalistic origin and considerable realistic importance.[41] Mass-energy amalgam extends to all forms of energy, leading to the 'shocking' concept of 'inertia of energy', which scientifically and synthetically a new science.[42] Relations are established between two conservations: of mass and of energy.[43] This realism is the result of the fusion of the two classical concepts at higher level.

This is a great conceptual development of the principles of *dialectical realism*.

Bachelard further makes the controversial statement that "efficacious thought proceeds in the direction of rationalism→ realism. Primacy belongs to rationalism, not to realism.[44] But rationalism itself is a stage and a condensation of realism. He considers realism 'too simple' a label. In fact rationalism is a reflection of realism. A certain period of realism gives rise to rationalism of higher order, which includes the previous realism. It is more like spiral path with its own negations and negations of negation.

"Thus the philosophy of contemporary science as it issued from the revolutions of the beginning of the century appears as a dialectic of enlightened rationalism and elaborated realism."[45] "Seen from the nuclear level, one might well say that matter evokes a neo-materialism in which substance and energy are interchangeable entities."[46] He and Eddington take the concept of matter to a higher level. He quotes Eddington as saying: "Matter is not a cause; it is an index." Bachelard adds further: "All exists together as the structure of space-time."[47]

This is very important statement, showing the higher spiral growth of materialism. That means *matter exists as space-time,* a great contribution of electromagnetism.

"The unifying formulas of general relativity are philosophical syntheses which reunite rationalism and realism."[48] Using his comparison of general relativity, we can say that the dualism of mind and body is placed in the context of electromagnetism. Synthesis and continuous spiral of rationalism, realism and materialism through dialectics reveal new realities.

NOTES

1. In, Paul Arthur Schilpp (ed.), *Albert Einstein: Philosopher-Scientist*, Open Court Publishing Company, Illinois, 2000.
2. Ibid, p. 7.
3. Ibid, p. 21.

4. D.P. Gribanov, "Einstein's Philosophical Worldview", in *Einstein and the Philosophical Problems of 20th Century Physics*, Progress Publishers, Moscow, 1983, p. 12.
5. Ernst Mach, from the essay: "The Economical Nature of Physical Enquiry", quoted in Wikipedia.
6. Ibid.
7. Lenin, *Materialism and Empirio-criticism*, Progress Publishers, Moscow, 1967, p. 132
8. Ibid, pp. 37-38.
9. Ibid, p. 47.
10. Ibid, Chapter 1.6, pp. 89-92.
11. Ibid, Ch 1.6.
12. Paul Arthur Schilpp (Ed.), op cit, p. 21.
13. Ibid, p. 25.
14. Ibid.
15. Ibid, pp. 25-27, emphasis added.
16. Ibid, p. 27.
17. Ibid.
18. Ibid, p. 33.
19. Ibid, p. 35.
20. Ibid.
21. Ibid, emphasis added.
22. Ibid, pp. 81-83, emphasis added.
23. Gaston Bachelard, "The Philosophic Dialectic of the Concepts of Relativity", in ibid, p. 568.
24. Ibid.
25. Ibid, pp. 568-69.
26. Ibid, p. 572, emphasis in the original.
27. Ibid.
28. Ibid, emphasis added.
29. Ibid, p. 573, emphasis in the original.
30. Ibid.
31. Ibid.
32. Ibid.
33. Ibid, p. 574.

34. Ibid.
35. Ibid, p. 575.
36. Ibid.
37. Ibid.
38. Ibid. , p. 576.
39. Ibid.
40. Ibid.
41. Ibid, p. 577.
42. Ibid, p. 578.
43. Ibid.
44. Ibid, p. 579.
45. Ibid.
46. Ibid.
47. Ibid.
48. Ibid.

4

Attitude of British and German Scientists

Attitudes of British and German physicists differed considerably because of several objective reasons. This is an interesting part of philosophical materialism based on concrete interpretation of sciences. Most British physicists in the late 19th century interpreted nature as if the laws of mechanics were valid at the microscopic level also. Electromagnetism could be interpreted in mechanical sense, and the laws of the observable bodies could be transferred as such to the molecules and atoms. Even Maxwell thought the physicists were better served by appealing to mechanical representation. They thought that an electromechanical representation of light was impossible.[1] To most British scientists the cathode rays were charged material molecules.[2]

Many German physicists regarded mechanistic bias of the British physicists as superficial and misleading. The Germans considered dependence on mechanics a limitation on mind rather than an aid to creative thinking.

This helped them grow, and at the same time, fall into subjective and idealist-imaginary concepts.

The book by Wheaton makes an interesting observation. The author describes one source of "this deeply ingrained cultural tendency in German physics" to be the prevalent atmosphere of idealist philosophy. The German speaking physicists were introduced to this atmosphere in their university days. An abstract interpretation of the natural processes was quite common in these countries. Consequently less emphasis was placed on material interpretation than in Britain.[4]

The 'material interpretation', if not taken to higher levels, can prove a hurdle to grasping the new realities, which do not exactly match with new levels of reality. The German emphasis on giving up mechanism can help grasping new reality, yet interpret them in agnostic manner philosophically.

A school of thought in the German speaking countries sought to follow *electromagnetic reductionism*. It sought to reformulate ideas of forces in ether solely in terms of forces in ether. "It was a form of electromagnetic reductionism and was heavily influenced by Kantian principles of epistemology."[5] On the other hand, Lorentz stated that all the interactions between matter and ether are mediated by (the hypothetical) electrons. Electrons are like particles but their mass and momentum are reflection of effect of electric force from ether. Mechanical properties of electrons are due to reaction between their charge and electric and magnetic fields.[6]

The concept of 'ether' as also its giving up led to a sprouting of imaginary and idealist-mechanical conceptualization. Though the problems were being solved at scientific levels, they became complicated and confusing at the philosophical ones, leading to a mix up of interpretations. Therefore, it is always essential to clarify the method in philosophy, even while dealing with science.

Speaking about the relations between light and electricity, Hertz claimed that everything could be fashioned from (reduced to) ether.[7] It provided explanation for matter and its properties.[8] Some scientists interpreted the assumptions of Hertz in an extreme form. They tried to establish the relationship between the continuous and the discontinuous in the electromagnetic field, and thus the mechanical concepts would be replaced. Wiechert and Wien felt "that the very concept of electron could be reduced to the idea of a form or structure in the electromagnetic medium."[9] The reductionists described their goal as the "electromagnetic picture."[10] The German and the British scientists moved due to their national characteristics towards wave and particle theories as the time passed! Wave theory as provided by Hertz and others was supposed to be more appropriate to the nature of the German scientists.[11] This should not mean that there was strict national division in scientific interpretations and that real discoveries on this basis were ignored.

Physics as practiced in Germany was much more willing to adopt formal principles without recourse to physical interpretation. By 1905, the word 'mechanics' was taken differently by many German scientists than those in Britain. "Influential voices had proclaimed that matter itself is only a construct of the mind, fashioned out of some ontologically significant electromagnetic forces that give rise to human perceptions of mass and extension."[12] The Germans were not tied to mechanistic outlook.

In the early 20th century Germany, there were two opposing theoretical programs regarding the interaction of matter and ether, trying to resolve their contradictions. The most widely accepted was the electromagnetic view of nature in various forms. Many of them wanted to dispense entirely with the *concept of matter*, and tried to reformulate mechanical properties only in terms of electrodynamics.

In time, the rapid developments in sciences led to the elimination, at least weakening, of the 'national' differences'. Science always does that and overcomes all the social differences through its discoveries!

NOTES

1. Bruce Wheaton, *The Tiger and the Shark: Empirical Roots of Wave-particle Dualism*, Cambridge University Press, 1992, p. 5.
2. Ibid.
3. Ibid, pp. 6-7.

4. Ibid, p. 7.
5. Ibid, p. 8.
6. Ibid.
7. Ibid.
8. Ibid.
9. Ibid.
10. Ibid, p. 9.
11. Ibid, pp. 10-11.
12. Ibid, p. 104.

5

Changes Brought About by Maxwell in Worldview

According to Einstein, "Newton's theory of motion, considered as a program for the whole of theoretical physics, received its first blow from Maxwell's theory of electricity."[1] It was found that electric and magnetic interactions between bodies were effected not by forces operating at a distance but by processes propagating through space at a finite speed. As per Faraday, a new kind of physical reality, that is, 'field' emerged. At first, attempt was made to interpret field as a mechanical state. But this did not work. Gradually, the electromagnetic field became a constituent of the physical reality. Hertz and Lorentz removed all the mechanical hurdles for the field.[2] It was shown that mass is not a constant quantity but depends on the energy content.

"In a more formal sense also Newton's mechanics prepared the way for the field theory. The application of Newton's mechanics to continuously distributed masses led inevitably to the discovery and application of partial differential equations, which in their turn provided the language for the laws of the field theory. In this formal respect Newton's conception of the differential law constitutes the first decisive step in the development which followed."[3]

Einstein says that "The belief in an external world independent of the perceiving subject is the basis of all natural science."[4] Sense perception gives only gives information of this external world ('physical reality') indirectly. Therefore we grasp the latter by speculative means. We must always be ready to change our notions ('axiomatic basis of physics').

The *greatest change in our conception of the structure of reality* ('the axiomatic basis of physics') was brought about by the works of Faraday and Maxwell in electromagnetism.

Einstein explains that according to Newton's system, physical reality is characterized by the concepts of space, time, material point, and force, that is, the reciprocal action of material points. In Newton's view, physical events are motions of material points in space, governed by fixed laws.[5] "The material point is our only mode of representing reality when dealing with changes taking place in it, the solitary representative of the real, in so far the real is capable of change.[6] "Perceptible bodies are obviously responsible for the concept of the material point..."[7] It was considered "as an analogue of mobile bodies, stripping these of the characteristics of extension, form, orientation in space, and all 'inward' qualities, leaving only inertia and translation and adding the concept of force." The material bodies led psychologically to the concept of material point, and had now themselves become a system of material points. It was an atomistic and mechanical interpretation, with motions of the points following Newton's laws of motion.[8]

Following this line of argument, *light also* came to be considered "as composed of material points". The question was raised even at that time as to what became of the material points of which light was composed, when the light is absorbed? Ponderable material and light came to be considered as composed of material points of different kinds.[9] With the passing of time, more and more *arbitrary* kinds of points and materials began to be added.

Newton had to devise differential quotients and propound total differential equations as form of laws of motion, "perhaps the greatest advance in thought that a single individual was ever privileged to make."[10] Partial differential equations (PDE) were necessary for the formulation of the mechanics of deformable bodies. *How* bodies are constructed out of material points was at the time of no importance.[11]

PDE became very important with the development of the wave theory of light in the 19th century. Light was explained as vibrations of ether, and here the PDE appeared as the natural expression of reality. Thus the continuous field appeared as the reflection of material reality along with the material point.[12]

"If the idea of physical reality had ceased to be purely atomic, it still remained for the time being purely *mechanistic;* people still tried to explain all events as the motion of inert masses..."[13] There seemed to be no other way of looking at the world.

Then came the great change, brought about by Faraday, Maxwell and Hertz.

Maxwell showed that light and electromagnetic phenomena could be expressed through his double system of differential equations. In them light and electromagnetism appear as dependent variables. Maxwell tried to fit in these equations through mechanical model.[14] By the turn of the century EM came to be considered as the ultimate reality, and its mechanical explanation had been given up. There began attempts to explain material points on the lines of the field theory.

According to Einstein, Maxwell brought about the following changes in our view of *nature of physical reality*. "... before Maxwell people conceived of physical reality—in so far as it is supposed to represent events in nature—as material points, whose changes consist exclusively of motions, which are subject to total differential equations (TDE). After Maxwell, they conceived physical reality as represented by continuous fields, not mechanically explicable, which are subject to partial differential equations. This change in the conception of reality is the most profound and fruitful one that has come to physics since Newton."[15]

In Lorentz's theory of electrons, field and electrical corpuscles appear side by side as elements of reality. The next developments are the special and general relativity, based on the field theory. They are based on ideas connected with field theories. But they have been unable to avoid the independent introduction of material points and total differential equations. The last and the most successful is the quantum mechanics, differing qualitatively from the Newtonian and Maxwellian systems. It does not claim to describe the physical reality itself, but "only the *probabilities* of the occurrence of a physical reality."[16]

"Dirac, to whom, in my opinion we owe the most perfect exposition, logically of this theory, rightly points out that it would probably be difficult, for example, to give a theoretical description of a photon such as would give enough information to enable one to decide whether it will pass a polarizer placed (obliquely) in its way or not."[17]

It was earlier thought that the "energetic world within the atom that lay beyond the scope of gravitation or electromagnetism"[18] was *safe from interference from 'outside'*. Here is a very important and interesting philosophical question needing detailed discussion. We will take it up again in the chapter on discussion. The point is that in a tangible and mechanistic world, (why do we consider the world always mechanistic? Why do we lose sight of dialectics?) there is a direct interference in the material processes. One thing or process is always based upon something else. But in the world of electromagnetism and quantum, they are not based upon something. They are independent entities. Therefore the possibilities of outside interference is much less or none at all. The outside here is the classical world. The moment we interfere, the process changes. Our interference changes the world, and we see the result. So we need to assess the extent and nature of interference and then conclude about the nature of the object, *the probability*. Instead of the object, it is the probability of the object that is important. We move from the domain of the fixed and the fixed motions to that of the continuous motions and conversions. We have to make final entry into the world of the probability and instability, and moving with them will give better view.

But there emerged some oddities. The first problem was the welding of electromagnetism with thermodynamics. Each was successful in its own right. Maxwell's electromagnetism elegantly explained the interweaving of electric and magnetic fields. The laws of thermodynamics explained heat engines, steam engines, properties of gases, chemical reactions etc.[19]

But the problem was it was considered that the space was filled with ether. The electromagnetic fields were thought to be strains or distortions in it. But this hypothetical ether seemed to have an insatiable appetite for heat. As a result the ordinary matter would surrender all its heat to the ether in form of electromagnetic vibrations of very high frequencies. Thus the matter would not remain stable in equilibrium with its surroundings.[20] As a result the ether had to be given up.

The other problem was the nature of the electromagnetic. The description of the *moving electric charges did not match with Newton's laws of motion.*

"Both these inconsistencies... concerned the nature of time."[21] The first, the conflict of electromagnetic theory and thermodynamics, grew out of an attempt to understand 'arrow of time', that is that the most physical processes had an inbuilt directionality. The second involved a clash between Newton's absolute time and the relativity of motion in electric charges.[22]

By the first decade of the 20th century, the first gave rise to quantum mechanics, the second to the theory of relativity.[23] Relativity meant that the appearance of the world to us depended upon our state of motion, and therefore it is relative. But it is not just motion which is relative; *space and time too are relative.*[24]

"For the 19th century scientists it was possible to believe

that physics would be complete if it could account for the forces that act between particles of matter, and the way those particles move under the action of the forces."[25] Everything boiled down to forces and motion. Later in the 20th century, the nature of space and time changed and they ceased to be background to the physical processes; they themselves became part of matter, *physical things* subject to the operation of the physical laws.

Experience, 'pure reason' and Reality

There has been an eternal antithesis between the empirical and the rational as the two inseparable polar opposites of knowledge. Einstein says pure logical thinking cannot yield any knowledge of the empirical world: all knowledge emanates from experience and ends in it.[26] Propositions arrived at by purely logical means are completely empty as regards reality.[27] "Because Galileo saw this, and particularly because he drummed it into the scientific world, he is the father of modern physics--indeed, of modern science altogether."[28]

What then is the function of *'pure reason'* in science? Einstein asked.[29] The conclusions must correspond to our experiences. Concepts and fundamental laws must be valid for the logical conclusions. Pure reason and experience have their own places in a theoretical system of physics.[30] Free inventions of human intellect cannot be justified either by the nature of the intellect or in other fashion a priori.[31]

NOTES

1. Albert Einstein, *Ideas and Opinions*, Rupa, 2019, p. 259.
2. Ibid.
3. Ibid, p. 260.
4. Ibid, p. 266.
5. Ibid, pp. 266-67.
6. Ibid, p. 267.
7. Ibid.

8. Ibid.
9. Ibid.
10. Ibid, pp. 267-68.
11. Ibid.
12. Ibid.
13. Ibid, emphasis in the original.
14. Ibid.
15. Albert Einstein, *Ideas*…etc, p. 269; see also, Paul Arthur Schilpp (Ed.), *Albert Einstein: Philosopher-Scientist*, Open Court Publishing Company, Illinois, 2000, pp. 257-58.
16. Albert Einstein, *Ideas*…etc, pp. 269-70.
17. Ibid, p. 270.
18. Paul Davies, *About Time: Einstein's Unfinished Revolution,* Simon Schuster, 1996, p. 14.
19. Ibid.
20. Ibid.
21. Ibid, p. 15.
22. Ibid.
23. Ibid.
24. Ibid.
25. Ibid.
26. Albert Einstein, *Ideas*…etc, p. 271.
27. Ibid.
28. Ibid.
29. Ibid.
30. Ibid, p. 272.
31. Ibid.

6

Lenin on Revolution in Natural Sciences and Concept of Matter

Lenin reached the conclusions *similar to those of Einstein* regarding the new developments in physics. In his famous work *Materialism and Empirio-criticism,* Lenin dealt in great detail with the nature and philosophical implications of the new developments in natural sciences in 19th-20th centuries. Among the points of debate was whether the concept of matter was outdated and whether 'matter' had 'disappeared' with the split in the atom.

Lenin reaches the very essence of the transition when he says: "...it is nevertheless beyond question that mechanics was a copy of real motions of moderate velocity, while *the new physics is a copy of real motions of enormous velocity*."[1] He hits the nail in this extremely profound statement, by discovering the very essence of transition, of the difference between the two kinds of realities, by pinpointing the dividing line between the classical and the new physics. Motions of 'enormous velocity', such as those of electromagnetism and light, constitute a qualitatively different kind of reality, whose study is the new physics.

Lenin here in very brief and in very few words explains the whole transition from the classical to the post-classical era in physics and philosophy. He simultaneously discovers the central axis, the time, in this transition. These concepts are much more applicable and relevant today.

Lenin quotes Joseph Diner-Denes, who directly compared the recent discoveries in science and physics (such as x-rays, Becquerel rays, radium, etc) to Engels' study in *Anti-Duhring*. He is quoted as saying: "In the most varied fields of natural science, new knowledge has been acquired, all of which tends towards that single point *which Engels desired to make clear*, namely, that in nature 'there are no irreconcilable contradictions, no forcibly fixed boundary lines and distinctions', and that if contradictions and distinctions are met with in nature, it is because we alone have introduced their rigidity and absoluteness into nature." "It was discovered, for instance, that light and electricity are only manifestations of one and the same force of nature."[2] This referred to the discovery made by James Clerk Maxwell. Lenin says further that each day it becomes more probable that chemical affinity is reduced to electrical processes. What was indestructible becomes destructible.[3]

"Quoting the opinion of one of the writers who regard the atom as only a condensation of the ether, the author exclaims: 'How brilliantly does this confirm the statement made by Engels thirty years ago that motion is the mode of existence of matter.'"[4] "All phenomena of nature are motion, and the differences between them lie only in the fact we human beings perceive this motion in different forms...It is as Engels said. Nature, like history, is subject to the dialectical laws of motion."[5] Lenin said prophetically that epistemological conclusions are being drawn from the discoveries, in which he was more interested. "These epistemological conclusions are of themselves so insistent that many physicists are already almost reaching them."[6]

He says further: "The recognition of theory as a copy, as an approximate copy of objective reality, *is materialism*."[7] He quotes Abel Rey's work *The Physical Theory of the Modern Physicists* (1907), who establishes the realistic and materialistic nature of new discoveries in physics.[8]

Knowing nothing of materialism, the Humean Rey had no conception of dialectics, of the difference between dialectical materialism and metaphysical materialism.[9] In presenting the views of other scientists, Rey expresses their indefiniteness and vacillations because of lack of firm materialist foundations. The crisis in physics led to a breakdown of old laws and basic principles, which often resulted in a rejection of the objective reality and in philosophical confusion.

Lenin says that materialism and idealism differ in their answers to the question regarding the *source* of our knowledge and of the relation of knowledge to the *physical* world. The question of matter, of atoms and electrons is a question that is related with the 'physical world'. What do we mean by saying, 'matter has disappeared'? "'Matter disappears' means that the limit within which we have hitherto known matter disappears and that our knowledge is penetrating deeper; properties of matter are likewise disappearing which formerly seemed absolute, immutable, and primary...and which are now revealed to be relative and characteristic only of certain states of matter. For the sole 'property' of matter with whose recognition philosophical materialism is bound up is the property of *being an objective reality*, of existing outside the mind."[10]

When the physicists say 'matter disappears', they refer to the investigation of the physical world to three ultimate concepts: matter, electricity and ether. Now the two latter remain. This is because it has become possible to reduce matter to electricity. Hence natural science leads to the 'unity of matter'. As we all know, the concept of 'ether' emerged as a working hypothesis, and disappeared as quickly when it was not needed and became superfluous.

The error of Machism (philosophy of Ernst Mach) is that it ignores this basis of philosophical materialism and the distinction between metaphysical and dialectical materialism.[11] To consider things as immutable is *metaphysics*, which means anti-dialectical.[12] Failure to differentiate between the two has led many physicists to the idealist, even mystic positions. Metaphysics is non-dialectical, even anti-dialectical, materialism.

J. Dietzgen, the humble worker, yet a profound philosophical thinker, emphasized that the subject matter of science is endless, even the smallest atom is immeasurable, inexhaustible, unknowable to the end. "Nature in all her parts has no beginning and no end."[13] Dialectical materialism insists on the objective reality. It also insists on the approximate and relative character of every scientific theory of the structure of matter and its properties. There are no absolute boundaries in nature. The transformation of the moving matter from one state to another is relative.[14]

"However bizarre from the standpoint of 'common sense' the transformation of imponderable ether into ponderable matter and vice versa may appear, however 'strange' may seem the absence of any other kind of mass in the electron save electromagnetic mass, however extraordinary may be the fact that the mechanical laws of motion are confined only to a single sphere of natural phenomena and are *subordinated to the more profound laws of electromagnetic phenomena*, and so forth—all this is but another corroboration of dialectical materialism. It is mainly because the physicists did not know dialectics that the new physics strayed into idealism. They combated metaphysical materialism and its one-sided 'mechanism', and in so doing threw out the baby with the bath-water."[15] Denying immutability of matter, they ended up by denying matter, that is, the objective material reality.[16]

They denied the most important basic laws, ending up by denying all objective laws in nature as convention, as necessary limitation and a logical necessity.[17] The essence of things is also relative. It expresses the degree of profundity of our knowledge of objects: yesterday it was the atoms, today electrons etc. These are dialectical milestones of human knowledge. "The electron is as *inexhaustible* as the atom, nature is infinite, but it infinitely *exists*."[18] It is the recognition of the nature's existence outside mind that distinguishes dialectical materialism from agnosticism and idealism.[19]

Phenomenalism and positivism follow subjective interpretation of the world, and therefore lead to reductionism.

Today too we find scientists and physicists straying into subjectivism, Kantianism and positivism while criticizing 'mechanism' of 19th century. While their critique of mechanism is useful and realistic, it strays somewhere into inconsistencies. For continuity and consistency, a dialectical approach is essential, as has been shown by the development of sciences over the last two centuries.

Bukharin's View on Science and Philosophy

Nikolai Bukharin was a great intellectual of Soviet Russia. Presently, we are not bothered about his political-ideological affiliations and other histories. What we are concerned with here is that he developed philosophy of natural sciences in the most trying conditions, contributing to the discussion on the nature of reality in the light of new discoveries in modern physics. His famous book *The Philosophical Arabesques* was written in the most difficult conditions in Stalin's jail. He was shot in 1938, a most tragic event.

Bukharin points to the philosophical and ideological confusion, crisis and distortions due to new developments in the natural sciences, particularly in physics. Lenin's work on Empirio-criticism explained the sprouting of idealism and agnosticism since 1908. "Matter has disappeared; equations remain", it was declared.[20] The whole controversy was in the context of the split in the atom. Bukharin deals with the developments in the sciences since the time of Lenin's book.

Bukharin mentions the further researches into the atom including Rutherford splitting it through bombarding it with streams of particles and discovery of its different components.

"This signified a great victory for materialism."[21] He says that the idea of the "ultimate building blocks of the universe" is anti-dialectical.[22] He criticizes the mechanistic materialism and shows how the developments confirm materialist dialectics. "Internal motion of atom" has been confirmed.[23]

Bukharin was among those materialist dialecticians, who recognized the deep impact of electromagnetism, relativity and quantum on philosophy. He said significantly that "it would of course be absurd if dialectical materialism were to tie its hands by proclaiming the 'picture of the world' achieved so far to be absolute truth."[24] Electromagnetism and subsequent discoveries have proved objective dialectics to be correct, he says.[25] "In modern physics this unity of the intermittent and continuous, with the interpenetration of opposites, has taken the form of the unity (and of the opposition in unity) of the particle and the wave."[26]

This is truly an important statement by an outstanding philosopher.

NOTES

1. V.I. Lenin, *Materialism and Empirio-criticism,* Moscow, 1967, p. 253, emphasis added.
2. Ibid, p. 238.
3. Ibid.
4. Ibid, p. 239.
5. Ibid.
6. Ibid, p. 253.
7. Ibid, emphasis added.
8. Ibid, p. 241, etc.
9. Ibid, p. 243.
10. Ibid, p. 248, emphasis in the original.
11. Ibid, pp. 248-49.
12. Ibid, p. 249.
13. Ibid.
14. Ibid.

15. Ibid, p. 250, emphasis added.
16. Ibid.
17. Ibid.
18. Ibid, emphasis in the original.
19. Ibid.
20. Nikolai Bukharin, *Philosophical Arabesques*, Aakar Books, Delhi, 2007, p. 200.
21. Ibid, p. 201.
22. Ibid, p. 202.
23. Ibid.
24. Ibid, p. 203.
25. Ibid.
26. Ibid.

7

Implications of EM and Quantum for Worldview

Two discoveries led to appearance of new world needing a reinterpretation. One was the intangible electromagnetism (EM) discovered through an analysis of the classical tangible objects and of the world created by them. Classical objects get connected with each other, not by the classical objects, but with *waves and particles moving at the speed of light*. The particles and waves constitute the fields that connect the *objects of the industrial vision*. What we need is a *post-industrial* vision.

With the discovery of electromagnetic field, we enter into a world of momentary particles and waves. *They transform the very structure of the world.* It is not possible anymore for our brain to deal with it in the old way. The new particles appear and disappear the same moment, *destabilizing the old world* and creating a new world of extreme velocities. They exist through their *non-existence,* and vice versa.

We also find that the tangible world is the product of the intangible EM, quanta, etc, and not the other way round.

The second one was the discovery of the quantum in 1900, leading to discovery of 'quantum', a new kind of particle. The concept of particle was drastically changed. The discovery was made on the basis of our simple and common day to day use of heat energy. Energy is continuous, not only in our everyday experience but also in classical theory, creating epistemological problems. Examples of energy are heat, light, temperature and so on.

It was thought that, as in case of gas, heating of the material will distribute energy equally among the particles or molecules. This is the classical notion. But while gas consists of atoms and molecules, *radiation (light etc) does not consist of them*. A new theory, a revolution in theory is called for.

The particle ceases to epistemologically, philosophically and materially to explain natural phenomena. It ceases to be a tool of cognition. Beginning with electromagnetism, 'particle comes out of the particle' and becomes free. At these levels, the particle is the product, rather than the constituent, of reality. At atomic and molecular levels, the particle creates many qualities but at post-classical and quantum levels, *it itself becomes a quality of space.*

It was found that the radiation consisted of several types of waves. Energy does not follow the pattern of distribution of energy among the gas molecules/atoms. In other words, energy is not equally distributed among the particles or atoms etc. What significance has this simple fact?

It emerged that energy is radiated as different frequencies of waves, as oscillators of a wide range. It was found by Max Planck in 1900 that emission of energy is broken up into pieces or packets, which he named 'quanta'. Otherwise there would be unbearable heat or catastrophic light (like x-rays or gamma rays etc) in our everyday life and explosions even!

Thermodynamics at the radiation changes drastically and qualitatively, giving rise to 'radiation-thermodynamics'. The 'equi-partition principle' is not applicable at this level, that is, the equal distribution of energy among the atoms and particles. Atoms/molecules are not mathematical points but finite objects with diameter etc.[1] In case of light and such other radiations, the situation is different. The waves or beams of energy do not affect each other's path and propagation. Each wave does not intensify and does not create unlimited intensity of energy. Each wave carries certain fixed amount of energy, depending on its wave length, fixed for each wavelength. Each wave has a precise amplitude, wavelength and frequency. These quantities are pinpointed. Therefore, the energy it carries is of a fixed amount, only this much, not more, not less.

Now, each wave carries a certain amount of energy divided into packets or 'quantum' (singular) or quanta (plural). The energy is transmitted in fixed packets. This prevents any catastrophe and 'overheating' of the system. Oscillators absorb and emit energy proportional to the size of their oscillation. The frequency of the wavelengths is fixed for each one of them.[2]

What Do We 'See'? EM and New World

There exists an entity diffused through space, modified by electromagnetism, acting upon bodies. It is the 'field'. According to Faraday, they are the bundles of lines, cobwebs, filling space around us (the 'Faraday Lines'). They carry force.[3] An object with electric charge distorts electromagnetic field. (Ibid) The world thus is no longer constituted of particles moving in space while time passes. A new 'actor', the field, enters the scene.[4]

This discovery needs *a modification of the structure of the world*. Electromagnetism explains most of the processes of the world.[5] Maxwell realizes that Faraday's lines tremble and undulate. The undulations move at the speed of light. This adds new dimensions to the material reality. That which moves at the speed of light is an altogether different entity. Only laws of relativity can explain them. It is a world moving at light speed, and therefore their mode of existence and structures must be qualitatively different. The structures cannot remain structures but must dissect into the constituents moving at light speed.

Light is nothing other than rapid trembling of Faraday lines. With the same stroke, electromagnetism showed what light is.[6] Color is frequency of electromagnetic waves that light is, and to 'see' is to perceive light, which is motion of Faraday lines.

Thus the space between two or more tangibles is filled with an exceedingly complicated structure, which is a world of its own.

'Something transports images': this is an exceedingly important aspect of reality. We see an object simply because of the vibrating lines in *between* it and our eyes. Rovelli gives the example of a child playing on the beach, both of whom we 'see'. We see them simply because "between them and ourselves there is this lake of vibrating lines which transport their image to us." Seeing is perceiving light.[7]

Thus the reality is combination of tangible and intangible. Without the intangible, the tangible would not have emerged and would have remained unseen. To 'see' means to get in contact with the image being transported. Between the two tangible objects, the field and the Faraday lines vibrate and carry/connect the two. Our eyes, retina, the equipments and gadgets catch these vibrations of images, and thus we see. That is how our image of the world, our outlook is formed. The tangible must get converted or dissociated into waves and particles before expressing itself, and reconvert itself into the former self. It is a transformation of the self/existence of one into another. In fact the tangible has to convert itself into numerous intermediaries in order to present itself. They vibrate if they are to express. *It is the vibrations that represent/ reflect tangible reality by transporting the latter.*

So what we see has a lot inside or behind which we are unable to see or catch! At least for the present. The waves and particles carry the images modified by the tangible objects and the intangible fields. It becomes difficult to 'really' know the real object, really difficult to know. It is the light, the 'F' undulations that bring the objects or the reflections from them to us. Then what the object is really like? To do so, we enter into a whole series of deeper investigations.

"The world is not made up of space + particles +

electromagnetic field + gravitational field. The world is made up of particles + fields, and nothing else..."[8] This means there is no need to add space as an extra element.[9] What Newton visualized as space *is actually a gravitational field, or the gravitational field is space.*

Our worldview has so far been determined by the space fixed and flat. This has changed, because now this space moves and moves at light speed, undulates and is subject to equations. Space is no longer separate from matter; the latter is submerged within the space. In fact space has been found to be 'material'. The solar system for example is supposed to be moving, 'rolling' in a vast sheet of gravitational space.

The existing picture of the world undergoes a change. Empty world is now a world full of rapid transformations, motions and energy conversions: it is a different world altogether dominated by high velocities. Sun and other stars bend the space around themselves. Light is simultaneously an electromagnetic wave and a swarm of photons, establishing a new reality of the *granularity* of all things including light.

Color is the speed at which 'F' lines vibrate. This is determined by the vibrations of electric charges emitting light.[10] In Newton's mechanics, an electron can revolve round its nucleus at *any* speed, and hence emit light at *any* frequency. Light emitted by an atom does not contain all the colors of light.[11]

In the electromagnetic world, energy radiates at fixed wave-lengths. Their velocities cannot be increased or decreased. Electrons can move in the atom only in fixed orbits. Any change in the orbit involves absorption or release of fixed energy. "The frequency at which the electron moves on these orbits determines the frequency of the emitted light..."[12] Only certain frequencies are allowed.

New interpretation to the processes in the space has to be given in order to grasp the world that lies there. The conclusion from Heisenberg is that the particles do not move, are not in motion, precisely speaking, *that is,* in the usual sense; *they emerge here, there and everywhere,* they pop up endlessly.[13]

Where Are Things Happening?

Peter Atkins asks, "Where is it that anything happens?"[14] He puts things simply that when we look around, we find that we exist in space and act in time. Till now the answer has been simple and a settled one. Social and natural sciences have studied and developed various kinds of space and time, particularly during the industrial age, which made space and time part and parcel of reality, of our life and consciousness.

Thus *modern consciousness* is the product of space and time as the condition of our existence, the industrial existence. *We exist in space and time.*

But the postmodern, post-industrial picture of world is different. There is a shift from space and time to space-time, to a world of waves and particles. Electromagnetism is the transitional state to this kind of world. Our consciousness has to face a state of shift from slow velocities and ordered processes to rapid changes high velocities. Processes inside our brain assume greater importance. *This is going to deeply affect the human development in future.* We were in a world where events happened one by one, and we grasped them as such. But now we are moving into a world where things/ processes 'happen' exceedingly rapidly and not 'one by one', not orderly, at least not in the sense of orderliness we are accustomed to. It is difficult to 'maintain' the world. We are, so to say, floating, *caught between two worlds*. Our consciousness is being molded by contradictory pictures of reality. In the new world, *time is the determining factor*. The nature of reality, thing and process is determined by the accelerating speeds and velocities. There is no fixed structure and relations between its constituents. *Classical structures are being demolished*. Reality, objectivity and matter mean increasingly rapid motions. The material forms progressively take on immaterial forms or lose forms entirely. We are moving towards a world *without forms.*

It is a world of high speeds and rapid conversions, which can be known only through information. They can only appear, can be seen, on screens etc but never directly. To be seen they must be converted into tangibility or screen information. The meaning of 'seeing' has changed for ever.

These events are incongruous with our body *but increasingly congruous with our mind.*

Philosophy has evolved over a terrain where idealism, materialism and other trends have battled in and over space and time. Therefore, time and space are simultaneously philosophical generalizations, validating concepts of idea and matter. We have treated the world as a stage of our actions, with space as background and acting in certain time lapse. We have treated our existence as a succession in time. *Existing philosophy is built on the stability of space and gradual, step by step development (flow) of time.* Great philosophers and philosophies did their job by delving deep into reality and idea, discovered essence and appearances, laws and categories of motion, related consciousness with matter. They had to take the help of tools of knowledge, categories and concepts to uncover inter-relations between different parts of the world. Both philosophy and science had to use tools of labor and knowledge to uncover reality. They also had to use speculations to approximate themselves with what may be found out there, for the endless inter-relations can only be abstracted/generalized.

Philosophy is a tool to grasp the slow-moving reality and aspects thereof, a response to the earthly motions matter, society and human beings. It is a science of generalizations, which bring forth aspects and their inter-connections. Philosophy is basically the reflection and product of this earth. We can reach essence only through appearances and phenomena, and this job has to be performed by philosophy, as also by the sciences. It needed thousands of years of philosophizing and scientific study to *reach/discover* the momentary quantum particle constituting the world and the universe, and the process continues. By philosophizing the tangible and the lighted, we have broken through, divided it, and a crossed beyond it, and synthesized a quite different world. We have entered for the first time the non-lighted world. So far we had been wandering in a lighted world *as if in the dark*! The lighted world we saw with too little light!! That is, we had to resort repeatedly to speculation and generalization.

This base or terrain has shifted now, and shifted tectonically. The mutual relations of space, time and matter have undergone massive change. To see or to understand is to anticipate the future.

How *Do* We Look at the New World?

We are now faced with the reality constituted by field, waves and particles. How does our brain relate with it and create new ideas? It is a world invisible. We use numerous gadgets and apparatuses to relate with this reality. It is through them and through their use in daily life that we draw certain conclusions and ideas about them, such as about electromagnetism, which is used in microwave, radio and other areas. Electromagnetism has become part of our daily life. Yet, we really do not know about electromagnetism as such, and *have not yet re-oriented our worldview*. But we are being forced to do so in the light of growing number of new post-classical discoveries.

The question remains as to really how electromagnetism, for example, helps create ideas, how does it reflect in our brains. One thing is clear, and that is that we reflect such a reality indirectly, through experiments and gadgets. They take on certain forms on the screens and in the apparatuses. We then reach certain conclusions about their existence. The subject-object relation is indirect, via certain conclusions about the reality. We cannot approach this material form directly in any case. We cannot 'see' it. This is a departure from what we experienced so far in our history. This needs a *different* philosophical approach. Our object of experience is *qualitatively different* from what history presented us.

An important feature of the new reality is that *we are not sure* of its permanent or stable existence. We are sure that a rock or a ball continues to exist even when we turn our back for certain period of time. But that does not apply here. There is a change in our relation with tangible object, time and space. There is no tangible object anymore.

Not only the object, the subject itself is constantly shifting, adjusting, being rendered transitory, and is being repeatedly constituted and reconstituted.

We cannot grasp the new realities using classical method. It is rightly stated by Richard Feynman that "Attempts to understand the motion of the electrons going around the nucleus by using mechanical laws... were a real failure..."[15] The motion of the electrons cannot be understood in the same way as the motion of the earth and other planets around the sun. The laws are entirely different, the philosophical approach, consequently, has to be different.

We transit from the *certainty* of reality to its uncertainty. This is a huge change in the ambience of the human beings, in which their ideas were formed. The ideas now accord with the shifting vantage points and changes in the frames of reference.

Newton's laws laid the foundations of mechanics, and also had puzzling philosophical implications later on.[16] According to Newton's laws, the behavior of a particle could be predicted on the basis of its interaction with other particle/s and forces acting upon it.[17] Then the future of every particle and of the universe itself could be precisely determined.

This view has today assumed the nature of mechanistic view of the world or of mechanistic materialism. It is outdated.

One of the greatest achievements of 19th century science was the demonstration that the electromagnetic radiation was in motion, '*field in flight*'.[18] In the early 20th century, light was seen as consisting of particles known as photons, the packets of *electromagnetic energy*. It is a particle of energy. It acts as the messenger particle, carrying a force between the originating and the receiving particles (electrons, nucleus, etc). "The photon is the messenger particle for the electromagnetic field, carrying the force between the interacting particles and travelling at the speed of light."[19]

In the sub-atomic domain, energy is not transmitted as in classical mechanics, that is continuously but indiscrete jumps (quanta). When two electric particles approach each other, they come under the material influence of EM fields and forces operating between them. The disturbance which one particle causes the other is transmitted through the field in form of photons. This is different from the continuous processes between the gravitating bodies like, say, the sun and the earth. The interaction between charged particles is a series of sudden impulses due to transfer of photons.[20] Thus the energy is not transmitted as in classical mechanics.

How do we form our ideas of the reality at this speed? Here we reach out to the reality in high motion, in the obvious motions beyond the capacity of the brain. By 'obvious' motion we mean that motion which we need not derive, need not conclude through our numerous experiences and experiments.

Here the motion is obvious, so much so that 'matter' almost 'ceases' to exist! This notion of matter does not fit in with our consciousness, and brain ceases to be the receptacle of the new idea moving at the speed of light. *We see motion but derive matter from derivations*. Motion is almost *the* reality. Calculations and mathematics play a crucial role in describing reality. We 'look' at matter through calculations of highly complicated nature. This is because the wave or the particle is not 'there' as it is, before our observation! It is an *accidental reality*, something that happens to exist only for the increasing divisions of a second or a micro-second!! Matter is transformed into energy, and it is energy we perceive and calculate. The field is full of transformations, most of them involving energy transformations. It is the information on motion that brings in reality to our consciousness.

The new reality connects *all bodies and forms* in the universe with fields, forces, waves, particles and so on moving predominantly at light-speed. It is only at this speed that such a connection can be established. It is the mechanical speed, which formed our worldview, not the light speed. Light speed lighted the mechanical bodies and their mechanical speeds to develop consciousness. What we now perceive is not the objects but their energy conversions. We deal with motions, not with matter or deal with matter only secondarily. We have to use calculations to determine the position of the particle and the frequencies of the waves.

In the world of electromagnetism, the tangible bodies get connected by a whole world of forces and motions, with which we are neither familiar nor habituated. We find it difficult to interpret philosophically and ontologically. Ontology is the study of what exists. Unless we are sure about existence, we can neither study nor develop epistemology.

Problem of Creation of Subjectivity

According to Paul Davies, "both the Stalinesque and Orwellian explanations are based on the common notion that there exists a 'seat of consciousness', a subject lurking somewhere in our brains like a spectator in a movie theater…" being fed on stream of sensory impressions.[21] In this view, a definite line can be drawn in time: the moment the sense data 'enter your consciousness'. "Unfortunately, such a picture of consciousness is almost totally discredited these days."[22] Dennett presents consciousness as involving a series of *processing and editing* functions, continually refining and updating the incoming data in parallel. As a result there is a smearing of *temporal relations*. The subject and the stream of data of events are created by many parallel streams of data processing.

In other words, there is no mechanical entry of data into

the brain, creating subjectivity. It is a dialectical process.

The problem here is that Dennett seems to entirely rule out the emergence and development of the subject. "Consciousness", he says, "is not the presentation of (possibly edited) data to a *mythical* subject (mind), but *is* the sum-total of the data streams taken together." The brain doesn't have to go through 'filling in' anything.[23] The problem here is that the subject has been proposed as 'mythical', while it is in reality an active opposite of what is coming from the outside as data. It receives the data, which today is processed or semi-processed. The brain is not a passive recipient of data but an active analyzer and synthesizer. Under the impact of the information revolution, the data is highly processed by the partially intelligent apparatuses and then fed into the mind.

There is another interesting aspect to the problem. The quantum world is more at par with the brain and its processes. Therefore at the molecular, atomic and quantum levels, there is a possibility of brain components, its cells and neurons as well as the electromagnetic currents inter-acting directly with the waves and the particles. This has nothing to do with mysticism and parapsychology, which are unscientific claims.

According to Paul Davies, nerve signals are physical things, subject to laws of physics. We cannot act on sensory information until we receive them. The incoming signals do not only inform us, but goad us into action: they have causative effect. The conscious subject is not a mere passive observer but an agent.[24]

Are Human Beings Capable of Understanding World?

This is a novel question that has cropped up in the wake of the EM revolution. The EM is forcing a reworking of all the questions regarding 'understanding', including its redefinition. Dirk Eidemuller unveils interesting aspects in the course of an absorbing discussion. Says he: "This is a very deep question. Niels Bohr once answered to that question, with regard to quantum physics: Yes, we will understand, but we will also learn anew what understanding means."[25]

This is a very important and intriguing epistemological question. With the transition to post-classical phase of science, philosophy raises new questions, and we have to redefine what is 'understanding'.

Eidemuller regards Bohr's following remark as probably the most important general philosophical insight: quantum physics forces us to reconsider what understanding actually means, showing limitation of our imagination. Quantum physics pushes us to a point where we have to accept that we cannot find any kind of visualization of what happens in nature anymore. "We can devise models for one phenomenon or another" but they may not apply in different circumstances."

Thus we have to devise models to help us see.

Then Eidemuller makes exceedingly crucial point: "And when you start thinking about why our mind is not able to imagine microscopic processes, you easily reach the conclusion that it is like that because evolution has not made us this way. Never in the history of our ancestors have microscopic phenomena been part of their sensory environment. So there has never been any need to develop structures of consciousness that would enable us to better understand the quantum world."[26]

This is very important, a crucial point. We have evolved in a particular way, habituated to observing tangible objects. Our body and mental structures are made, structured accordingly. Our mind and body is incapable of sensing microscopic processes. It is a big task to convert our consciousness into grasping microscopic, electromagnetic and quantum phenomena.

We begin to work with mathematical anticipation, calculations and models and visualizations. For the last 2 to 3 centuries, human consciousness has developed in a deterministic manner, dealing with tangible things and processes. Our philosophical views have developed under such an influence. With EM we begin to make transition to indeterministic ideas. Discoveries in the field of quantum science further strengthen this trend.

Eidemuller gives the examples of Kant, Laplace and dialectical materialism as those of determinism. In passing he makes a surprise comment on social theory of Marxism: enlargement of dialectical materialism, the philosophical foundation of Marxism, "whose authors incomprehensibly enlarge the concept of determinism to the development of societies."[27] He does not explain why it is 'incomprehensible'. The founders of Marxism, Marx and Engels have explained in detail the objective laws of origin and development of society, treating it as an object of scientific investigation. For the first time society was treated as if in precise laboratory conditions. This was the novelty of treating nature and society as one. We will not go into further details and controversies here.

NOTES

1. George Gamow, *Thirty Years That Shook Physics: The Story of Quantum Theory*, Dover Publications, New York, 1985, p. 14.
2. Manjit Kumar, *Quantum*, Hachette India, 2009, p. 25.
3. Carlo Rovelli, *Reality is Not What it Seems*, Penguin Books, UK, 2017, p. 41.
4. Ibid, p. 43.
5. Ibid, p. 44.
6. Ibid, p. 45.
7. Ibid, p. 46.
8. Ibid, p. 65.
9. Ibid.
10. Ibid, p. 97.
11. Ibid.
12. Ibid, p. 98.
13. Ibid, p. 100.
14. Consult Peter Atkins, *Galileo's Finger: The Ten Great Ideas of*

Science, Oxford University Press, 2003, Chapter 9, p. 275, etc.

15. Richard P. Feynman, *QED: The Strange Theory of Light and Matter*, Universities Press, 1999, p. 5.
16. See, John Gribbin, *In Search of Schroedinger's Cat*, Wildwood House, London, 1984, p. 9.
17. Ibid.
18. Peter Atkins, *Galileo's Finger... etc*, p. 180, emphasis added.
19. Ibid, p. 181.
20. Jagjit Singh, *Space and Time Waltz*, Publications and Information Directorate and Wiley Eastern Ltd, New Delhi, 1995, pp. 83-84.
21. Paul Davies, *About Time: Einstein's Unfinished Revolution*, Simon Schuster, 1996, p. 268.
22. Ibid.
23. Quoted in ibid, p. 269. The first emphasis is ours while the second one is in the original.
24. Ibid, p. 272.
25. Dirk Eidemuller, "Quantum physics, philosophy, and understanding our world". Talk with Dr Vera Koester on 6 December 2016, in *Chemviews Magazine*, from Google.
26. Ibid.
27. Ibid.

8

Kantian Agnosticism and Transition to Electromagnetism

The discovery of electromagnetism gave rise to serious debates on philosophical questions, including on the nature of reality. There is a certain revival of *apriorism,* empiricism and even agnosticism as a trend in the light of the new discoveries.

We have to go back a little into the background to properly understand why this has happened, though this is not the only trend.

The Irish philosopher George Berkeley (1685-1753) was a proponent of *sensationalism,* considering sensations as the only source of knowledge. Sensationalism was a double weapon, leading both to materialism and idealism: it was materialism if the sensations kept touch with matter (material reality); it turned idealist if it lost the touch. The materialist trend included Locke, Holbach, Helvetius and Feuerbach. Berkeley interpreted sensations in an idealist manner. He absolutized the sensations, considering them as the *only* source of knowledge and as the sole reality.

Many of Berkeley's philosophical formulations were repeated 200 years later by the positivists and Machists. Berkeley had denied the objective existence of the real world, treating our ideas, feelings and sensations as objects of our knowledge. What we perceive is not things but our own sensations ('ideas'). We know things only through our sensations, which with Berkeley, are the only reality.

According to Berkeley, things are 'group of ideas'.[1] "To exist means to be perceived", as per Berkeley.[2] This leads directly to solipsism. Addressing the materialists he said: "But, say you, though the ideas themselves do not exist without the mind, yet there may be things like them, whereof they are copies or resemblances: which things exist without the mind, in an unthinking substance. I answer, an idea can be like nothing but an idea."[3]

Machists were direct precursors of Berkeley. Machists, also known as 'empirio-symbolists', considered sensations not as copies of reality but as signs and symbols of things.[4] Sensations, empirio-symbolism and 'economy of thought' were some of the expressions taken over by the positivists, Machists and neo-Kantians from idealism of two centuries old empiricism.

The 18th century agnostics David Hume (1711-76) and Immanuel Kant (1724-1804) were among the important sources of Machism. Hume says that once we raise doubt on the existence of the external world, we cannot allow the existence of a 'supreme being' outside of us.[5] Causes of sensations, perceptions etc cannot be deduced from experience. It is impossible to prove that perceptions in our mind are caused by external objects. It is as impossible to prove that perceptions are produced by mind itself. Source of knowledge is unknown. Reality is a stream of impressions with unknown and unknowable sources.[6]

Says Mach: "Bodies do not produce sensations, but complexes of elements (complexes of sensations) make up bodies."[7] If to the physicist, bodies appear the real entities, abiding existences, while the 'elements' are regarded as transitory appearances, the physicist forgets that all bodies are thought- symbols for complexes of sensations. Thus the 'bodies' are for Mach mere 'thought-symbols' and no more. This is a completely imaginary and idealist thinking/philosophy.[8]

Discovery of electromagnetism and field, and the

consequent beginning of transition from classical to post-classical reality generated serious philosophical debates about the nature of 'reality', objectivity and subjectivity. The great German philosopher Kant had, and continues to have, deep influence on the post-classical and quantum scientists. There are reasons for this. Kant was also a great scientist deeply influenced by Newton. He was an outstanding geologist too. His nebular thesis is well-known. But most of all he is known for dividing the reality into two parts: knowable and unknowable. We are not going into the details of his philosophy but will mention only the relevant points.

Discoveries in electromagnetism, quantum and relativity have only strengthened the interest in the Kantian agnosticism. While he advocated importance of experience of the material world, his emphasis on the transcendental and 'beyond experience' things and aspects have resurfaced with the realization that experiments and experimental truths are increasingly not possible in the world of waves and particles. Experiments are not able to establish new truths/realities. Kantian '*apriorism*' has gained strength with assumptions in particle and wave physics, where mathematics and calculations are resorted to establish the truth of reality. Observations fail and there is a 'loss' of experience.

Thus Kantian philosophy is truly torn between idealism and materialism. Its materialism is also dual and uncertain, unable to clinch the question of reality. Kant advanced the theory of 'things in themselves', of the things which could be known. As such he was a materialist. He was a great scientist, and as such worked to unravel the objective processes deep within the world.

Yet part of 'things in themselves' remained 'themselves', and could not be known. Consequently, Kant advocated agnosticism with increasing force. It is a surprise that science in Kant co-existed with agnosticism, creating an inner tension in his philosophy. This was also because of his *apriorism*, according to which certain realities can only be thought out much in advance, without their being real.

These are the contradictions of Kantian philosophy. Some of the physical, electromagnetic and quantum philosophies resort to transcendentalism and *apriorism*, not because their discoveries and theories are wrong, but because they try to generalize (one-sidedly philosophize) the discoveries. Speculation begins as soon as science withdraws from investigations, strengthening agnosticism and certain mysticism. EM, quantum, etc have to assume and presume a lot, and therefore there is an easy recourse to *apriorism*.

Philosophers of modern physics have to increasingly face the problem of *constitution of objectivity*, rather than its being merely given.[9] Therefore a transcendental approach in the spirit of Kant is presented as relevant. At the same time the true challenge is not to force modern physics into a static version of Kant's philosophy but to provide flexibility to Kantian method.

Bitbol *et al* differentiate between 'transcendent' and 'transcendental'. Both the words mean 'exceeding experience'. Bitbol *et al* say transcendent and transcendental somehow point to opposite directions. Exceeding can be achieved in two ways. A transcendent *object* exceeds experience in so far as it 'allegedly exists *beyond* experience'. By contrast, a transcendental structure exceeds experience because it is a *background precondition* of experience. A transcendent object is supposed to wait for us 'out there' and is indifferent to our intervention. By contrast in transcendental preconditions, we decide the rules and methods, and select the phenomena, and treat the process 'as if' something is there, as they 'appear'. Here we constitute them.[10]

Electromagnetism and quantum world provide the terrain for both transcendent and transcendental experience. It is a journey into the unknown, and we really transcend the tangible world. The world beyond is subject to unlimited interpretations. Our mental world, used to depend on certain solidity, is free-floating, so to say, in that world. Therefore only the uncertain philosophical interpretation seemingly come to our rescue. Yet this leads us nowhere except back to the solidity of the existing world. We find ourselves interpreting wrongly.

The transcendental realities of space, time (actually space-time) and quantum relativity defy our attempts to define and delineate the new world. Unless the world outlook is firmly rooted upon the inexhaustible unity of the material world, we will not be able to interpret it. Transcendentalism does not help us to reveal the truth of 'real reality'. One has at least to agree to recognize the objective reality of the world of rapid velocities, which increasingly interacts with our consciousness. To that extent our consciousness is modified.

Shaking of the Old

What has shaken the classical physical and philosophical bases of our understanding? It is the overthrow of the concepts of absolute space, absolute time and absolute velocity.[11] They were the very basis of the classical-Newtonian human existence. Referring to Michelson experiment, Bachelard asks in an interesting way: Is so little required to 'shake' the universe of spatiality? Can a single experiment annihilate three centuries of rational thought? "Yes, a single decimal sufficed... to 'make all nature sing'".[12]

Referring to Kantian philosophy, Bachelard says *apriori* intuition and real experience are attributable to the success of the concept of absoluteness. "This double success of a raw realism and over-simple intuitionism seems spurious."[13] This double philosophy must be replaced by a *dialectical philosophy*.[14] The new philosophy of science will prove to be a critical philosophy more subtle and synthetic than the Kantian philosophy.[15] Thus 'raw' realism appears 'spurious' in the context of the post-classical events.

The scientific revolution brought about by electromagnetism, Michelson experiment, quantum revolution and relativity has destabilized science by *destabilizing the subject*. The position of absolute space affirms immobility of the subject and mechanical motions. It is also "the residence of an unconditioned subject in the centre of conditional relations."[16] The subject is a fixed one relative to the objects. The objects move in the space and therefore can be fixed in terms of time. It is in mutually determined and fixed relations that the subject and the object move and evolve. The subject views the objects as in fixed motions, giving a mechanical impression.

Remarking on concepts in general, Einstein says the "concepts have reference to sensible experience, but they are never, in a logical sense, deducible from them. For this reason I have never been able to understand the quest of the *a priori* in the Kantian sense".[17]

'Mind-like' Quality at Particle/Field Level

"The content of our consciousness is then some part of this overall process. It is thus implied that in some sense *a rudimentary mind-like quality is present even at the level of particle physics*, and that as we go to subtler levels, this mind-like quality *becomes stronger* and more developed."[18] The relationship is increasingly participatory in the quantum world and its events.

Thus the subject goes deeper and becomes more enriched at deeper levels of reality.

The *subject*, in the process, becomes a 'mental pole' opposed to the physical pole, as represented by the electromagnetic and quantum phenomena and fields/forces. This subject thus is qualitatively different from that of the classical reality. According to Bohm and Hiley[19], "even an electron has at least a rudimentary mental pole, represented mathematically by the quantum potential."[20]

In materialism and idealism, one pole is a mere function or

aspect of the other. Before the advent of quantum theory, we would have denied that the knowledge of matter could have a mental pole. Such a pole would have enabled it to participate with mind in the objective process. The knowledge of matter has changed in a way that supports participation of both the poles in the world events.[21]

Classical physics only reflected the objective structure of the human observer. There was no room for his mental processes, which were only an extension of the objective process.

This is an extremely crucial point, *characterizing a transition of historical importance*. It is the growing *unity and merger* of the natural forces with those of human brain. It is the first time that brain can interact with objectively existing processes in a way that they form a unity. *The realities of the mutual relation of object and the subject get blurred here.*

Kant, Hegel, Marx and Engels: Dialectics vs. Metaphysics and End of Philosophy

It is surprising that the physicists and scientists, particularly the German scientists, often refer to Immanuel Kant to interpret the results of the new developments in electromagnetism and quantum sciences, yet they fail even to mention giants of philosophers like Hegel, Feuerbach, Marx, Engels, Lenin and many others. They particularly fail to mention the great dialecticians and their dialectical method, so very essential for present-day physics and philosophy. Perhaps political-ideological considerations come in between! If this is so, it very unfortunate for natural sciences and quantum physics, particularly for drawing philosophical conclusions from it.

Let us keep aside the ideological considerations and concentrate purely on philosophy. It cannot be denied that Hegel was an unparalleled philosopher, who provided the methodology to understand and interpret the world as no other philosopher did. We will not go into the details of his philosophy or method except referring to them in certain contexts only.

Engels says that "nature is the proof of dialectics"[22], and that its (nature's) development has proved that it works dialectically, and not metaphysically. Yet, he correctly points out, the naturalists who have learnt to think dialectically are far and few in between.[23] It is in this dialectical spirit that the German philosophy has worked. Kant began his career by resolving the stable solar system of Newton and its eternal duration into the result of a historic process of formation of the sun and all the planets and out of a rotating nebulous mass.[24] His theory was later established mathematically by Laplace. After that, spectroscope proved the existence of the nebular gasses.

According to Engels, "this new German philosophy culminated in the Hegelian system".[25] For the first time it became possible to represent the whole world as a process, as in constant motion and development. "It was now the task of the intellect to follow the gradual march of this process through all its devious ways, and to trace out the inner law running through all its apparently accidental phenomenon."[26] Hegel could not solve the problem, but no single individual could.

Hegel was an idealist, for whom things and their evolution were only realized pictures of the 'Idea'. This way of thinking turned everything upside down.

This fundamental contradiction of German idealist philosophy led inevitably back to materialism, but on a higher plane. The new plane was materialism with motion and dialectics as its core. Modern materialism is based upon the latest discoveries in the sciences. Nature is shown to consist of various kinds of motions, and thus reality and motion assume concrete forms, with the evolution of natural sciences. Newton, Linnaeus, Darwin, others were able to prove existence of motions and their laws in concrete spheres.

Engels makes an extra-ordinary *discovery* in that the "modern materialism is essentially dialectic, and *no longer needs any philosophy* standing above other sciences."[27] This is a great discovery, which helps us to understand the impact of natural sciences on our world outlook. Each special science investigates particular field of reality, and therefore a special science dealing with it is unnecessary. "Everything else is subsumed in the positive science of nature and history."[28]

Engels says in the rough draft of the Introduction that: "The Hegelian system was the last and most consummate form of philosophy, in so far as the latter is represented as a special science superior to every other. *All philosophy collapsed with this system*."[29] What remains is the dialectical method of thinking. Philosophy and all the sciences are now required to discover the laws of motion of this process of transformation. "And this was the legacy which Hegelian philosophy bequeathed to its successors."[30]

Engels makes a crucial point elsewhere. It is that modern materialism "is no longer a philosophy at all, but simply *a world outlook*" which has to be applied to the real sciences.[31] Philosophy is sublated, and both overcome and preserved here; it is overcome as regards its form and preserved as regards its real content.[32]

So philosophy is replaced by world outlook or worldview, applicable to every branch of science.

With the growing discussions as a result of the growing crises of the classical sciences, a section of scientists tend to acquire mystical and mythical interpretations to the growing shifts to momentary and rapid events. These events are similar to mental processes or nearer to them. Hence there are greater tendencies towards transcendentalism. This emphasis on the transcendent seeks to mystify and make amorphous the world picture. A transcendental and agnostic interpretation or such emphasis on the Kantian philosophy comes handy in the transition from the tangible to the intangible. Over-emphasis is laid on the so-called 'experience', beyond which the existence of the world is 'doubtful'. Difficulty in knowing the real nature of things is presented as impossibility to know, with certain tolerance for agnosticism, a criticism of which is avoided.

Beginning of Philosophy as Worldview

Complicating the matter is the fact that science is replacing philosophy as a tool to explain the world. Philosophy is known as the 'science of sciences', which it was when the sciences were only evolving. Philosophy essentially is an abstraction of the gist, substance or the abstract of the existence. The essence or the abstract ignores the concreteness and reaches the depth of matter, existence and idea. Philosophy does not mainly concern with what we see but with the essence of existence.

Sciences have given meaning to our observation, ever going deeper into material existence. The industrial revolution has 'concretized' the existence: the abstract has become concrete in stages. Science establishes concrete relations between reality and our consciousness, making speculations superfluous. Consequently, our consciousness develops differently.

Today, worldview and even philosophy are re-emerging as the post-classical world poses new questions about existence. Older philosophical problems are re-appearing in newer forms.

NOTES

1. A.O. Sternin, *Lenin's Materialism and Empirio-criticism*, Progress Publishers, Moscow, 1988, p. 20.
2. Ibid.
3. From, "A Treatise Concerning the Principles of Human Knowledge", quoted in Sternin, p. 20.
4. Ibid, p. 21.
5. Ibid, p. 23.
6. Ibid, pp. 23-24.
7. Ernst Mach, *The Analysis of Sensations*, Introductory Remarks:

Anti-Metaphysical, Chapter I, Part 13, from Marxists.org/Google.

8. Ibid.
9. See, 'About this book', an Introduction to *Constituting Objectivity: Transcendental Perspectives on Modern Physics*, ed. by Bitbol, Kerszberg, Petitot, 2009, from Google.
10. Ibid.
11. Gaston Bachelard, "The Philosophic Dialectic of the Concepts of Relativity", in *Albert Einstein: Philosopher-Scientist*, ed. by Paul Arthur Schilpp, Open Court Pub Co, USA, p. 568.
12. Ibid.
13. Ibid.
14. Ibid.
15. Ibid.
16. Ibid.
17. Albert Einstein, *Ideas and Opinions*, Rupa, 2019, p. 278.
18. D. Bohm and B.J. Hiley, *The Undivided Universe*, Routledge, 1993, p. 386, emphasis added.
19. Ibid, p. 387.
20. Ibid.
21. See, ibid, p. 388.
22. Frederick Engels, *Anti-Duhring*, PPH, New Delhi, p. 31.
23. Ibid.
24. Ibid.
25. Ibid.
26. Ibid, p. 32.
27. Ibid, pp. 33-34, emphasis added.
28. Ibid.
29. Ibid, p. 32, Footnote.
30. Ibid.
31. Ibid, p. 159, emphasis added.
32. Ibid.

9

Einstein and Dialectics of Evolution of Field

Einstein explains that in Newtonian mechanics, space and time play the part of carrier or frame for events in physics. Events are described by space coordinates and time. Matter consists of 'material points'; their motions constitute physical events. The second role of space and time consists in being an 'inertial system'. Physical reality consisted of space and time, and of material points moving with respect to the space and time.[1]

This view was overcome with the concept of field. In classical physics the concept of field was *auxiliary* to continuous matter. It was characteristic of the field that it occurred only *within* the ponderable matter, describing a state of matter. Where there was no matter, no field existed.[2]

But in the first quarter of 19th century, light began to be regarded as wave-field, analogous to mechanical vibration field in an elastic solid body. Thus field existed in 'empty space' *without* the ponderable matter.

This created a paradoxical situation. Field was considered subject to mechanical interpretation, presupposing presence of matter. Ether was assumed to be the form of matter. "*The emancipation of the field concept from the assumption of its association with a mechanical carrier*" is an interesting development in the history of physical thought.[3] Researches by Faraday and Maxwell took the field *beyond* mechanical concepts. By introducing field concept, Maxwell predicted the existence of electromagnetic waves, which had essential identity with light waves. Optics thus was absorbed by electrodynamics. *The field concept gradually became independent of the mechanical framework of the classical physics.*[4]

At first it taken for granted that the electromagnetic fields were states of ether, which were then interpreted mechanically. But gradually this interpretation had to be given up in stages. Still, by the turn of the century electromagnetism continued to be states of ether.[5] Its giving up led to the special theory of relativity.

The investigations of Lorentz explained the EM and optical processes within the ponderables on the assumption that the influence of the ponderable matter on the electric field and vice versa "is solely to the fact that the constituent particles of matter carry electrical charges, which share the motion of the particles."[6]

When Lorentz began his scientific work, Maxwell's electromagnetism had already won out. But there was a problem in it of fundamental principles. Though the field concept displaced concept of action at a distance, the electric and magnetic fields had not yet been conceived as primary independent entities. They were just considered states of 'ponderable matter'.[7] Matter was considered carrier of field.

Lorentz provided a fundamental clarification. He hypothesized that "The seat of the electromagnetic field is empty space."[8] This field is generated by atomistic electric charges, upon which then the field exerts force. The only connection between the electromagnetic field and matter are the electric charges attached to atomistic particles of matter. "For the latter Newton's law of motion holds."[9]

Newtonian Mechanics, Einstein and Physical Worldview

An important property of our experience is its temporal order. This kind of order leads to a mental conception of subjective time, and ordering of our impressions. The subjective time then leads via the concept of the bodily object and of space to the concept of objective time.[10] The bodily object is directly connected with complexes of sense experiences. One property which is characteristic of the notion of 'bodily object' is the property providing that we coordinate to it an existence independent of (subjective) time, and independent of the fact that it is perceived by our senses. We do this despite the fact that we perceive temporal changes in it. Poincare emphasizes that we identify two kinds of changes in the object: 'change of state', and 'change of position'.[11]

There are objects which within certain area of perception do not show change in state nor in position; this is a fundamental point for the formation of concept of space and even of the concept of the 'bodily object'. "The very name *geometry* indicates that the concept of space *is psychologically connected with the earth as an ever present body of reference.*"[12]

The notion of 'space', which preceded scientific geometry, changed our mental concept "of the relations of positions of bodily objects into the notion of the position of these bodily objects in 'space'".[13] In the geometry of the Greeks, space plays only a qualitative role, as the position of the bodies is given, but is not described through numbers.[14] Physical notion of space is also tied to the existence of rigid bodies. The concept of space is useful but not indispensable for geometry proper, that is, for the formulation of rules about relative positions of rigid bodies. In contrast to this, the concept of objective time is linked with the concept of spatial continuum. *Classical mechanics is impossible without the concept of objective time.*[15]

Objective time involves two postulates:

1. Objective local time interconnected by temporal sequence of experiences, done with the 'clock'. Clock is 'a periodically recurring closed system'.[16]
2. Extension of the concept of objective time to the events in whole of space: the idea of local time is extended to the idea of time in physics.[17]

Our everyday experience *neglects* the time of propagation of light. We are used to a failure to differentiate between 'simultaneously *seen*' and 'simultaneously *happening*'. Consequently, the difference between time and local time is blurred.[18]

The lack of definiteness adhering to the classical time, was veiled by axiomatic representation of space and time as given independently of our sense experience. An error of believing that these notions are essential may constitute serious danger to the progress of science. It was fortunate that for mechanics that lack of definiteness of objective time remained hidden from philosophers. "Full of confidence in the real meaning of the space-time construction, they developed the foundations of mechanics...."[19] These foundations consisted of the following concepts and laws: 1. Concept of a material point. 2. Law of inertia. 3. Laws of motion. 4. Laws of force. "These fundamental laws, together with Newton's law for the gravitational force, form the basis of the mechanics of celestial bodies."[20]

Einstein has rightly brought out in focus the ambience in which have been brought up and developed through the ages. We are so used to these laws that we find it very difficult to turn away from them. Even the scientists find it difficult.

Although classical mechanics fails as a foundation of physics today, *it still occupies the center of thinking in physics,* as also in philosophy. This is because a new foundation has not yet been built properly. The notion of 'material point' is fundamental for mechanics. In such a situation, if we try to develop mechanics of a bodily object which cannot be treated as a material point, how can we treat the body as built up of material points? What forces operate between them?[21] Only answers to these questions can describe the mechanical world. These material points and their laws are invariable for mechanics.

Classical mechanism leads us to an atomistic construction of matter. Therefore it is an error to assume that theory comes inductively from experience. "Even the great Newton could not free himself from this error ('*Hypotheses non fingo*'—'I make no hypotheses').[22] Newton was the first creator of a comprehensible and workable theoretical system of physics, points out Einstein. Newton "still believed that the basic concepts and laws of his system could be derived from experience."[23] This is the meaning of his abovementioned saying. Concepts of mass, inertia, force, their laws etc seemed to be drawn from experience. Consequently gravitation too was derived from experience. Newton was not comfortable with 'absolute space' and 'absolute rest'. There was nothing to experience in it. He was also not comfortable with 'action at a distance'.[24]

Mechanics leads *naturally* to the concept of matter. Science tried to save itself from being lost hopelessly in the atomistic line of thought.[25] "The mechanics of a system is determined if its potential energy is given as a function of its configuration."[26]

In order to save itself from getting hopelessly lost in atomism, science had to adopt the following path of development. It adopted two modes of application of mechanics: One, mechanics of a system is determined if its potential energy is treated as the function of its configuration.

Two, the second method avoids the sub-division of matter down to the 'real' material points. Instead it takes to the mechanics of the 'continuous media'. They are based on hydrodynamic theory and the theory of elasticity of the solid bodies.

These theories *avoid* introduction of material points. These formal tools created through partial differential equations.[27]

These two modes of mechanics belong to what Einstein terms as '*phenomenological physics*'. It makes as much use of concepts close to experience as possible, such as heat, electricity, light etc. But for this very reason, it has to give up the 'unity of foundation'. Their mutual relation could only be solved empirically. These experiences have been generalized, giving a one-sided picture of the world we live in. Many physicists thought the ultimate aim of physics could be obtained purely inductively from experience because of closeness of concepts to experience.[28]

Einstein says that from the point of view of theory of knowledge, Stuart Mill and Ernst Mach took their stand generally on this ground. But here it has to be pointed out that for Mach experience was detached from reality and experience. For him all bodies are 'thought symbols' for complexes of elements or 'complexes of sensations'. So his ground is not experience but abstract thought. Therefore, his theory of knowledge was more subjective and idealistic.

"In my view, the greatest achievement of Newton's mechanics lies in the fact that its consistent application has led beyond this *phenomenological point of view*, particularly in the field of heat phenomena."[29] The experiences of the Newtonian realities helped us to go beyond them, or at least prepare grounds for going beyond.

Newton's mechanics connected equations of the states of matter and gave the logical connection of phenomena, which from the point of view of direct experience had nothing whatever to do with one another. The phenomenological interpretation on the other hand gave a mechanical interpretation of the thermodynamic ideas and led to the discovery of the limits of classical theory of heat.

It was with heat energy and experiments related with it that the quantum theories ultimately evolved.

The kinetic theory of gases surpassed the 'phenomenological physics' regarding logical unity of the latter's base. It also produced definite values for the magnitudes of atoms and molecules. Constructively speculative character of the entities of the coordination of atomic and material points was clear. Nobody could 'directly perceive' an atom. Laws concerning variables like temperature, pressure, speed etc were derived from fundamental ideas through a series of complicated calculations. Physics *originally* was more phenomenological. It later came to be based upon Newtonian mechanics of atoms and molecules. Thus these entities were removed from direct experiments and experiences. Thus transformed, Newton's mechanics as applied to the unobservable atoms and molecules became increasingly self-contradictory. This created further basis for removal from direct observation and experiments. Newton's mechanics itself created the bases for far more uniform and applicable, that were to appear in the post-classical worldview.[30]

Newton's mechanics failed to explain optical and electrical phenomena. Newton tried to reduce light to the motion of material points in his corpuscular theory of light. It was an extension of mechanical approach. But it had to be endlessly modified, showing its unreal character, and ultimately abandoned. "For the theoretical conception of electric and magnetic phenomena one introduced, again, masses of a special kind..."[31] Applying Newton's gravitational force, action at a distance was assumed between these masses. But this lacked the fundamental property of inertia. The whole picture was obscure. This progress has to be paid by increasing the complexity of forces acting between the electrical masses in motion.

The electric field theory of Faraday and Maxwell represented *the most profound transformation* of the foundations of physics since Newton.[32] As per Einstein this growing constructive speculation "*increased the distance* between the foundation of the theory and sense experiences." We may add here "and the concrete experiments."[33] "The existence of the field manifests itself, indeed, only when electrically charged bodies are introduced into it."[34] The electric masses are places of non-vanishing divergence of electric field. "Light waves appear as undulatory electromagnetic field processes in space."[35]

As a result, in this theory, *field took over the position occupied in Newton's mechanics by material points*. This applied to the EM fields in empty space.[36]

Initially the theory was quite unsatisfactory for the *interior* of matter. Here Lorentz found a way to theory of bodies in motion. He showed that everywhere, including in the interior of the ponderable bodies, the seat of field is the empty space. Elementary particles carry electric charges as part of the electromagnetic phenomena. They are subject to the forces of the tangible bodies, and on the other hand, generate field. These elementary particles follow Newton's laws of motion for material points, he said.[37]

On this basis Lorentz obtained a *synthesis* of Newton's mechanics with Maxwell's field theory. "The weakness of this theory lies in the fact that it tried to determine the phenomena by a combination of partial differential equations (Maxwell's field equations for empty space) and total differential equations (equations of motion of points)".[38] The procedure was unnatural. The theory had to assume "*finite dimensions for the particles*". (Ibid, emphasis added.)This became necessary in order to prevent the electromagnetic field at the surface from becoming infinitely large. Besides, the theory failed to explain the tremendous force holding the electric charges in individual particles.[39]

Ultimately, the theory of particles with infinite dimensions won out, and physics charted out on a new path of negation of the classical laws.

Logical Method in Physics

According to Einstein, "There is no inductive method which could lead to the fundamental concepts of physics... Logical thinking is necessarily deductive...".[40] In his opinion, failure to grasp this led many scientists of 19th century to "basic philosophical error."[41] Deductive logic is based upon hypothetical concepts and axioms. He gives as examples the perpetual motion, Galileo's inertia and theory of relativity.

The Maxwell-Lorentz theory validated the EM equations for empty space, and for light travel 'in space' at a constant speed. For a number of considerations "it was necessary to raise to the rank of a principle the validity of the law of constancy of light velocity for all the inertial frames."[42] "The failure of classical mechanics, as revealed by the theory of relativity, is connected with the finite speed of light (its not being infinite)".[43]

Mechanics Works with Infinite Entities

"Physics constitutes a logical system of thought…whose basis cannot be distilled, as it were, from experience by an inductive method, but can only be arrived at by free invention. The justification (truth content) of the system rests in the verification of the derived propositions by sense experiences, whereby the relations of the latter to the former can only be comprehended intuitively." Logical basis is becoming increasingly simpler. "The logical basis departs more and more from the facts of experience", and the path of our thought from basis to derived concepts correlating with sense experiences *becomes harder and longer*.[44] He tries to demonstrate that the concepts of bodily objects, space, subjective and objective time, etc are inter-connected and related with experience. Space and time are independent in classical mechanics. The concept of bodily object is replaced with that of the material point: thus *mechanics becomes atomistic*. Light and electricity displace mechanics as the basis of all physics. Field theory of electricity emerges, and then physics itself is based upon field. Attempts to overcome mechanics lead to theory of relativity.[45]

"Science is the attempt to make the chaotic diversity of our sense-experience correspond to a logically uniform system of thought." Individual experiences must correspond to theoretical structure.[46]

"With the progress of science, the realm of physics has so expanded that it seems to be limited only by the limitations of the method itself."[47]

Einstein, Kant and Experience

It is clear that Einstein assumes the existence of an external and objectively existing world largely independent of the observer *as the basis of science*. Henry Margenau comments that in Einstein there is *an identification of the external world with the physical world*. At the same time, there is a difference between an essence of reality and what appears to be.[48] "Indeed there is implied a three-fold distinction between an *external world*, the observer's *perception of that external world*, and our *notions* of it..."[49]

Einstein is quoted to state: "The belief in an external world independent of the perceiving subject is the basis of all natural science. Since, however, sense perception only gives information of this external world or of 'physical reality' indirectly, we can only grasp the latter by speculative means. It follows from this that our notions of physical reality can never be final. We must always be ready to change these notions—that is to say, the axiomatic basis of physics—in order to do justice to perceived facts..."[50]

Here Einstein clearly provides a materialist and a dialectical interpretation of the world: an independent world, sense perception giving the information, but indirectly, we grasp the reality by drawing general conclusions or through generalizations, our notions of physical reality can never be final, and we must be ready change our notions in the light of the new perceived facts, and even be ready to change the axiomatic basis of our notions, such as in physics. The axiomatic basis is drawn from abstractions and generalization from perceptions and other forms of observations.

Margenau correctly says the following in his interpretation of this quotation:

- there is an identification of the physical reality with the external world;
- there is an insistence upon the difference between essence of reality and its appearance;

- there is a three-fold distinction between an external world, observer's perception of that external world and "our notions of it";
- axiomatic structure of physics is not drawn or abstracted from sensory perception.

But Margenau makes at least two problematic and controversial interpretive statements in this regard. He says:

That there is a 'trace' of *rationalism* here in Einstein. The fact is that it is not a 'trace' of rationalism; it is a full blown rationalism based upon recognition of physical reality and material realism.

To this end, Margenau refers to the use of the word 'indirect', and says this is an 'innocent' word. He is right. He is also right in stating that the word 'indirect' "hides a multitude of epistemological problems" which the scientists generally ignore.[51] The author is correct as to the presentation of the problems facing the scientists.

But his interpretation is misplaced because of a number of reasons.

Having said this, Margenau reaches makes strange conclusion that Einstein was reared in Kantian tradition, and espoused the unknowable 'thing-in-itself'! This is what he states: "Having been reared in the Kantian tradition Einstein conceivably espouses a *Ding an sich* which is intrinsically unknowable."[52] *But this is not true!* Einstein nowhere gives an impression to the effect that he believed in the 'thing-in-itself'. In fact he has contradicted the Kantian approach clearly, as we have seen earlier. Commenting on the 'pre-scientific concept of space'[53], Einstein says that the "concepts have reference to sensible experience, but they are never, in a *logical sense,* deducible from them. For this reason I have never been able to understand the quest of the *a priori* in the Kantian sense."[54]

It is also not true that Einstein's concept of external world independent of the observer is problematical. This assumption flows from regarding Einstein being a Kantian. What Einstein states *clearly* is that science studies an external world which exists objectively and independently. In his detailed criticism of the quantum theories, in particular its philosophical implications regarding the objective existence, Einstein finds himself opposing any view which denies objectivity. The 'meaning of externality' is not a metaphysical question, as Margenau assumes, but materialist philosophical one, and as characterized by science. Margenau himself states that Einstein demarcates himself from the positivist and empiricist schools of philosophy.[55]

In support of his mystic interpretation of Einstein, Margenau quotes the following from Einstein: "Behind the tireless efforts of the investigator there lurks a stronger, more mysterious drive: it is existence and reality that one wishes to comprehend. But one shrinks from the use of such words, for one soon gets into difficulties when one has to explain what is really meant by 'reality' and by 'comprehend' in a such a general statement."[56] But here Einstein is already dealing with the problem of interpretation of 'reality' and 'comprehension' in the light of new developments in sciences. And he nowhere seems to shirk from it.

Margenau's discussion raises the pertinent question as to "the exact manner in which theory represents physical reality".[57] This question needs proper discussion as it is a complicated one. He says that it is clear from "Einstein's statements and writings that he was an opponent of the view according to which theory *copies* reality."[58] On this point Einstein takes the issue with British empiricism.

In fact, it is not theory that 'copies' reality, and certainly not directly; it is the initial reflections of the surrounding world and its things that are reflected in our brain as perceptions and ideas. Reflection, perception, reaction, etc are almost 'copies' of the material reality in all its variety.

With theory, reflection of the world moves towards the essence of the object and of the objective reality. It is not the copy of the surface, but it certainly is the 'copy' as an abstraction of the deeper meanings and generalizations.

British empiricism and scientific dialectical materialism are two different things. Empiricism is a mechanical approach to the concrete world, which is unable to catch the motions in the objective world, and therefore unable to take a qualitatively new turn. The changes can only be negotiated if dialectical method is used which recognizes constant transformations and qualitative changes in nature.

Einstein is stated to have said that the central recognition of relativity is that geometry is a construct of intellect, while Newton regarded geometry as a set of descriptive propositions flowing from physical experience. Only then the 'time-honored notions of time and space' can be 'tampered with'.[59]

Now, there is no contradiction here. Einstein has not 'tampered' with the notions mentioned. He only showed their obsolescence with new discoveries. He showed that geometry is as much the product of reality as of the intellect. Geometry on the earth is one thing; geometry in motion, that too at high speeds is another.

On pure reason and experience, Einstein says: "We have thus assigned to pure reason and experience their places in a theoretical system of physics. The structure of the system is the work of pure reason; the empirical contents and their mutual relations must find their representation in the conclusions of the theory."[60] That is the sole value of justification of the system and theory. He clarifies that free inventions of intellect "cannot be justified either by the nature of that intellect or in any fashion *a priori*".[61] He says further on[62] that experience remains the sole criterion of the physical utility of a mathematical construction. The creative principle resides in mathematics. So, in a certain sense, "pure thought can grasp reality".[63]

So what Einstein is talking about is taking thought process and abstraction to higher levels, even while it representing reality and experience.

Two points in this context need to be raised: 1. 'Copy' of the surrounding world in our brain is not a dead one but an active one. Brain is an active organism, which actively and pro-actively reflects things outside, analyzing and synthesizing them. It is able to 'know' and understand what it reflects, unlike the dead mirror. Therefore, the expression 'mirror image' in case of the brain has an active meaning. Even the initial reflection is an active one.

2. The concept of 'experience' is both passive and active, direct and indirect. Experience is an expression for our interaction with the outside world. In direct experience, we physically interact with the tangible object. There may be varieties of more indirect interaction, using tools and apparatuses.

With the new developments in sciences, there has been *a growing gulf between the observer and the observed*, increasing the role of concepts and hypotheses, calculations, mathematics, speculations and propositions, suggestions, leading to a growing role for worldview and philosophy, etc. He also states the following in this connection: The 'fictitious' character of the fundamentals of scientific theory "is steadily gaining ground from the fact that the distance in thought between the fundamental concepts and laws on one side and, on the other, the conclusions which have to be brought into relation with our experience grows larger and larger..."[64] He uses the word 'fictitious' to those concepts which are no longer applicable.

This has been well referred to by Einstein. We anticipate more about what is possible. Observations about electromagnetism, quantum and relativity are highly involved and indirect. There is controversy about what exactly we observe, and how. The highly controversial point is that when we 'observe', we interact with the object observed. As a result, the object is changed, which result we then anticipate and/or speculate and then conceptualize.

This also is 'experience', but of an entirely different kind, a conceptual experience, one about the deeper processes and essences. Therefore, it would be an error to mystify it. There is a tendency among the scientists to detach 'experience' from actual material, physical world, and abstractize it. The deeper we enter this world, greater is our distance from the surface reality, the greater our indirect experiences and conclusions. Field, gravity, waves, particles, etc are 'out there', but not in the form we 'observe' them as they are, but through our *interaction* with them at different level and in different forms. In this way, we 'know' them but not in the way that we know the tangibles. They exist in a form where our classical laws break down and others take over.

Einstein also rejects Mach's proposals on the absolute space. Though Einstein expresses his indebtedness to Ernst Mach for many concepts, he criticizes the latter for reverting back to mechanical interpretation when faced with the need to give it up. "To get round the notion of unobservable absolute space, Mach tries to save the laws of mechanics by substituting for an acceleration with respect to absolute space an acceleration relative to the inertial system moving with the center of mass of all masses in the universe."[65] Einstein rejected this concept completely because it amounted to accepting a universal frame of reference and required action at a distance, which in turn presupposed "universal simultaneity which is operationally absurd. By this chain of logical reduction does the suggestion of Mach finally destroy itself."[66]

NOTES

1. Albert Einstein, *Ideas and Opinions*, Rupa Publications, 2019, pp. 366-67.
2. Ibid, p. 367.
3. Ibid, p. 368, emphasis added.
4. Ibid.
5. Ibid, pp. 368-69.
6. Ibid, p. 369.

7. Ibid, p. 74.
8. Ibid.
9. Ibid.
10. Ibid, p. 295.
11. Ibid, pp. 295-96.
12. Ibid, pp. 296-97, emphasis added.
13. Ibid, p. 297.
14. Ibid.
15. Ibid, p. 298.
16. Ibid.
17. Ibid.
18. Ibid, p. 299.
19. Ibid.
20. Ibid, p. 300.
21. Ibid.
22. Ibid, p. 301.
23. Ibid.
24. Ibid, based on p. 301.
25. Ibid.
26. Ibid.
27. Ibid, based on pp. 301-02.
28. Ibid, pp. 302-03.
29. Ibid, p. 303.
30. Ibid, based on p. 303.
31. Ibid, p. 304.
32. Ibid, pp. 304-05.
33. Ibid, p. 305, emphasis added.
34. Ibid.
35. Ibid.
36. Ibid.
37. Ibid.
38. Ibid, p. 306.
39. Ibid.
40. Ibid, p. 307.
41. Ibid.

42. Ibid.
43. Ibid, p. 313.
44. Ibid, p. 322.
45. Ibid, p. 323.
46. Ibid.
47. Ibid, p. 324.
48. Henry Margenau, "Einstein's Conception of Reality", in *Albert Einstein: Philosopher-Scientist*, ed. by Paul Arthur Schilpp, Open Court Pub Co, USA, pp. 248-49.
49. Ibid, p. 249.
50. Ibid, p. 248; Albert Einstein, *Ideas and Opinions*, p. 266.
51. Ibid, *Albert Einstein: Philosopher-Scientist*, p. 249.
52. Ibid.
53. Albert Einstein, *Ideas and Opinions*, p. 277.
54. Ibid, p. 278.
55. *Albert Einstein: Philosopher-Scientist*, p. 249.
56. Ibid.
57. Ibid, p. 250.
58. Ibid, emphasis in the original.
59. Margenau, in *Albert Einstein: Philosopher-Scientist*, p. 250.
60. *Ideas*... etc, p. 272.
61. Ibid.
62. Ibid, p. 274.
63. Ibid.
64. Ibid, pp. 272-73.
65. Margenau, in *Albert Einstein: Philosopher-Scientist*, p. 251.
66. Ibid, p. 252.

10

Characteristics of Mechanical (Mechanistic) Philosophy and Problems of Quantity-Quality Conversions

We have become habituated to a world, where there is enormous diversity of things, whose inter-relations can be reduced to certain limited and definite framework of laws. These laws and basic features were considered absolute and final, and therefore the world picture and view was considered complete; changes took place only within this framework, not outside. Thought, fashioned in these conditions, was unprepared for sudden and drastic changes in the basic conceptions of the world. It has nothing to do with agnosticism or *apriorism*, because *everything* is supposed to have been known and explained.

The fundamental entities existing in this world framework have qualities that define their *mode of being* or 'mode of existence'. They have fixed and limited physical and mathematical existence, leading to a concept of qualities fixed for all time. Changes are mostly quantitative, with some qualitative changes, without affecting the world order, concept of reality and of matter, both physical and philosophical. Fundamental qualitative changes in the laws are generally not possible. Physical laws are often expressed as quantitative changes. Within the *mechanistic limits,* predominantly quantitative changes are possible. Consequently, further qualitative changes will only take the system beyond the mechanical limits.

Further developments in sciences have brought about many changes. The historical development of physics, such as in electromagnetism, quantum theory and relativity have changed the basic assumptions of the mechanistic philosophy.

Following are some of the essential characteristics of mechanical (mechanistic) materialism, as developed in physics.

The enormous diversity of things in the world can be completely reduced to effects of some basic laws and their framework, considered absolute and final.[1] They will reduce themselves to quantitative relations. The reality is fixed and explainable according to these laws and their physical/ mathematical scheme. Any changes will generally be quantitative, not qualitative, because that will only shake the foundations of reality.[2]

The historical development continuously contradicts the fixed assumptions of physical and scientific laws.

"The field concept, the concept of quantitative changes that lead to qualitative changes, the concepts of chance and statistical law" etc bring about specific changes in the conceptual structure of physics and revolutionary changes in the general framework of science because they are always relative and limited. Today the limits of its validity are being discovered. The possibility of change is always open.[3]

For example Newton's laws of motion regarded as absolute and final have reached their limits with the discovery of the quantum and relativity. The 'absolute' and 'final' are converted into *philosophical* categories of fixed nature.[4]

The assumption of the final and absolute character of any theory contradicts the basic spirit of scientific method itself, which requires that every feature be subjected to further and continuous enquiries.[5]

David Bohm says[6] that "the above arguments do not prove that a mechanistic philosophy is definitely wrong." It is just that "we have not just found the true absolute and final theory". This is a muddled and controversial assumption. At the same time, he correctly points out that "it may well be worth our while to consider points of view that go outside the limits of a mechanistic philosophy."[7]

The point is that every philosophy or assumption has its historical limits, at first revealing new levels of reality, and then its limitations. At this limit the theory becomes mechanical if it persists with its assumptions despite new realities.

At the same time, a mechanical theory itself has dialectical motion of its own, its inherent motion. Its limits are shown by new developments. The theory is mechanical if it explains itself with things outside itself. It is motion-based or dialectical if it is inherently motion-based.

Newton's first law is mechanical in the sense it needs an external force to propel it. It then becomes flowing and freely moving (dialectical) for infinity because of its own inner source. The whole of Newton becomes mechanical in the post-classical period simply because its basic assumptions based upon the tangible objects disappear into non-tangible objects, such as in electromagnetism, where the particle (point) is not solid/tangible. Besides, the motion is not of laid-back kind and orderly but converting immediately into one another.

While moving beyond the mechanical world, we come across the atomic theory of matter. The atom has disclosed increasing number of qualities and details of *a moving substructure.*[8] These qualities show no sign of exhaustion. Electrons, protons, etc have further motions of their own. Their motions are guided by quantum-mechanical laws, going beyond mechanical limits. Then came the discoveries regarding the structure of electrons, protons etc, consisting of particles such as mesons, hyperons etc. The mechanics of their motions are not yet clearly understood. "Still later came the realization that because these latter particles can be 'created', 'destroyed', and transformed into each other, they too are likely to have a further structure that is related to the motions of some still deeper-lying kinds of entities..."[9]

The substructures of the moving matter are themselves in high speeds and rapid motions. "An essential characteristic of the rich and highly interconnected substructure of moving matter..."[10] is that not only do the quantitative characteristics continually change but also that the basic qualities defining the mode of existence can change fundamentally. "Thus further research into the structure of matter has not only shown what is...an unlimited variety of qualities", but that all these qualities are subject to fundamental transformations.[11]

There are inexhaustible *depths* in the properties and qualities of matter.[12] Lenin says in *Materialism and Empirio-criticism* that "matter is inexhaustible'.[13] Experiments show there are levels within levels of smaller and smaller kinds of entities. Each of them constitutes substructure of the entity above, and each explains the motions and qualities above. The qualities also depend upon the background in which they come into being. According to Bohm, in physics, research has not emphasized this aspect as much as it should have. The introduction of various fields like electromagnetic, gravitational, mesonic (meson related), etc represents the background for these processes.[14] The mode of existence of the fields requires that they be defined over broad regions of space. They enter into the definition of basic characteristics of the fundamental particles.[15] These fields are highly excited, and can give rise to qualitative changes in the particles; particles in turn can impact the fields.[16] At the deeper levels, both are probably opposite sides of the same a general entity.[17] It could be a new kind of entity acting either like a field or a particle under certain circumstances.

The next step in physics may reveal the inadequacy of the procedure of going through level after level of smaller and smaller particles, perhaps connected with each other by fields. "Instead, we may find that the background enters in a very fundamental way even into the definition of the conditions of existence of the new kinds of basic entities..."[18]

We cannot decide it *a priori*. It may in future become difficult to apply the concept of a 'thing'.[19] If there are no 'things', how to formulate the laws of nature? Our mind is habituated to 'thing' or 'things', to which our thought hangs on. Such a thing has to have some degree of stability and autonomy in its mode of existence; it should preserve its identity at least for some duration.

The problem of observability or non-observability of quantity and its conversion into quality arises here as a crucial element of theory of knowledge. It is a novel problem. "To bring out the methodological role of this principle, it is essential to determine that such and such quantity precisely is not observable in principle." The question of the appropriate place of field in electromagnetism is also related with it.[20]

The qualitative infinity of nature provides a framework, within which concepts of chance and necessity are two interconnected aspects of the same process.

Niels Bohr in his 35 year long debate with Einstein regarding the nature of objectivity, clarifies certain ambiguous aspects of the new reality. Bohr states that the main point under debate was the attitude to be taken to the discoveries at the beginning of the century. Planck's discovery of the universal quantum of action "revealed a feature of atomicity in the laws of nature going far beyond the old doctrine of limited divisibility of matter...".[21] Bohr says that there is problem with the expression of Einstein, Podolsky and Rosen regarding what they call 'without in any way disturbing the system'.[22]

Here there are stages of the 'system'. *In earlier conditions,* we do not on the whole disturb the system; we can leave it intact, as it is after the act of observation and experiment. But now there are increasing number of systems which we cannot 'leave as it is'. They are in rapid motions. Besides, when we observe, they undergo a change, and we do not 'return' to them undisturbed; they even do not exist on our return.

The debates on the epistemology of the observational

problems with the transition to post-classical physics, and philosophy, continues to be a major problem.

NOTES

1. David Bohm, *Causality and Chance in Modern Physics*, Routledge, London, 1984, p. 130.
2. Ibid, p. 131.
3. Ibid.
4. Ibid, p. 132.
5. Ibid.
6. Ibid.
7. Ibid.
8. Ibid, p. 137.
9. Ibid.
10. Ibid.
11. Ibid, p. 138.
12. Ibid.
13. Lenin, *Materialism and Empirio-criticism*, Moscow, 1962.
14. Bohm, *Causality*... etc, p. 138.
15. Ibid.
16. Ibid.
17. Ibid.
18. Ibid, pp. 138-39.
19. Ibid, p. 140.
20. M.E. Omelyanovsky, *Dialectics in Modern Physics*, Progress Publishers, Moscow, 1979, p. 109.
21. Niels Bohr, "Discussion with Einstein on epistemological problems in atomic physics", in *Albert Einstein: Philosopher-Scientist*, ed. by Paul Arthur Schilpp, Open Court Pub Co, USA, 2000, p. 201.
22. Ibid, p. 234.

11
Discussion and Conclusions

It is clear from the discussions in the chapters that with electromagnetism, we have entered qualitatively new domains of reality or into new reality itself. We find it very difficult to grasp its nature and to form our ideas accordingly. The new reality does not fit in with our existing concepts, which we have to rework. Human being has been working with tangible reality, a reality which can be seen, touched, heard, smelt, etc. Even at the microscopic levels, we can see the outlines of the object (e.g. bacteria) and we can interpret those levels by extending our experience. Therefore, our worldview basically has been created in a world constituted by the tangible objects and processes.

Electromagnetism is a transitional phenomenon on way to quantum reality and relativity, a link, which considerably expands the new world picture. It is very difficult, next to impossible, to grasp and accept this reality because it is a world of exceedingly rapid transformations and very high velocities. How do we relate ourselves with that world? This is a crucial cognitive question of new problem in the theory of knowledge. How is the 'subject' changed in relation to momentary existence/phenomenon at high velocities? And is the 'object' an easy matter for us to comprehend? What is the relation of the subject to a high speed objectively existing world? Can the subject created at slow speeds comprehend events at light speed or near light speed? Can such a subject 'see' it? These are some of the new and crucial problems.

Does *matter* disappear or goes deeper at these speeds? This is another crucial question. In fact it is a basic question of philosophy.

The existing subject has been created over the millennia through gradual processes with intricate dialectics and step by step transformations consequent upon changes in the nature of material objects / processes. The existing subject takes highly involved routes to reach the changing objective reality.

With the new developments in sciences, there is *a growing gulf between the observer and the observed,* increasing the role of concepts, hypotheses and calculations, leading to a growing role for worldview and philosophy.

It is to be noted that *the role of time factor* has increased *as never before.*

Re-emergence of Philosophy: No Place for Agnosticism

As we have already mentioned, with the growth and development of natural sciences in the 19th century, philosophy as a 'science of sciences', as generalization of the concrete lost its importance and became superficial in many senses. With the transition of physics and sciences to electromagnetism, quantum and relativity, as also because of several other discoveries, the questions relating to the nature of world, reality and existence have re-emerged. The problems of the interpretation of the world and of tracing the relations of matter and idea, even of defining the nature of matter, have resurfaced. Physics, and sciences in general, are having to deal with these questions inevitably at some point or the other of their development.

It is surprising that many scientists are influenced deeply by the philosophy of Immanuel Kant. Of course there are reasons for it. Yet, it is rather difficult to understand why there is so widespread a Kantian influence. Reference to Kant does not lead to anywhere in the present context. Neither his method nor his philosophy is help in this great transition.

Kantianism and neo-Kantianism only lead to agnosticism and mysticism.

It is also surprising that the great dialectician and the German philosopher of the highest order Georg Hegel is hardly ever mentioned, if at all! And philosophers like Marx and Engels do not find mention at all. Electromagnetism and quantum sciences are the fields where motions and changes are exceedingly rapid. It is in order of things that the dialectical changes should draw inspiration from these great philosophers of change and dialectics, who in many ways foresaw the future developments. Hegel seems to have anticipated at least some of the changes mentioned in the quantum. Engels deeply studied the relationship between natural sciences and philosophy. Lenin defended matter against attempts to dissolve it. He defended physics and its materialist interpretation.

It is really unfortunate that scientific interpretations often fall into agnosticism and mysticism. That is why they take recourse to *apriorism* of Kant. It is very easy philosophically to go back to Kant whenever a vast field of the unknown opens out with the new discoveries in the sciences.

The new discoveries have strengthened dialectics as a science and as method. Scientists have often unconsciously applied the dialectical method, as in the case of EM discoveries. Einstein has done it so well.

Electromagnetism as Worldview: Concept of Energy

There are considerable differences in the way mechanics and electromagnetism conceptualize energy. In the former, energy is defined in terms of *force* and *work,* more as a description of the *past* of given body or system. Moreover, in the mechanical framework energy is ascribed to matter, i.e., one speaks of the energy *of a body*.

On the other hand, in the electromagnetic picture, energy assumes a form localized *directly* in the field; in other words, *it is part of the field*.

Furthermore, in electromagnetism energy is *no longer a property of an object*, but some kind of *extensive quantity in space*. Electromagnetic worldview thus is qualitatively different from worldview evolved by the traditional physics.[1]

This article in the abovementioned citation deals with the problems faced by teachers while teaching the concept of energy in the classical and electromagnetic modes. Though related with teaching, it involves the problem of the transition of the worldview, which has been dealt with very well.

In the historical development of physics, quite often we find a *resignification* of old concepts in the discovery / invention of new concepts. We try to find new meanings of the old concepts but we also try to fit the new developments *within* the framework of the old ones. Electromagnetism is also a glaring example, which has gone through several adjustments of the worldview. This also has happened with the concept of energy.

Max Jammer highlights some important aspects of this change as follows: In Poynting's theory of energy flow, transport of energy is no longer confined to conductors, the surrounding space is the arena where energy moves. Energy, disjoined from matter, raised its ontological status from a mere accident of a mechanical or physical system to the *autonomous* rank of independent existence, and matter *ceased to be* the indispensable vehicle for its transport. As a result of this 'emancipatory change' or reification of energy, the idea that only differences in energy are of physical significance had to be abandoned and an absolute magnitude had to be ascribed to energy.[2]

We reach a reality which is not fashioned by tangible matter but by energy pure and simple. How to cognize it?

Mindset of Electromagnetism

The new image of the world consisting of field and electromagnetism conveys *a very different mindset compared to the 'force and work' framework*. Despite its importance, the electromagnetic way of conceptualizing energy is rarely present in our thought and is yet to become common and a habit.

Even when dealing with electromagnetism (EM), we tend to follow classical worldview and philosophical approach. We take the field/EM as something flowing between the immediate material objects. We take them to be 'currents' flowing, in the common parlance, something within our control. At slightly deeper levels we try to break up the EM into tangible particles and try to look for 'atoms'. We fail to grasp that it is a different world.

At deeper levels, we interpret EM as electrostatics, the part of theory dealing with charges *at rest*, without mentioning the reference frames. Their state of rest *suppresses* the action of time, and one has the feeling that one is dealing with an *eternal world*, a problem of worldview.

One normally omits the information that two charges cannot remain at rest by themselves. After electric field and force, one introduces the potential energy[3], the energy of an object because of its position.

The symbols tend to emphasize properties of a *mechanical body*. However, *charges and bodies are very different things*. Moreover, the previously *static* charges acquire *kinetic energy*. The sudden transformation of *static point-like charges* into *moving bodies* appear at the most *ad hoc* and arbitrary. They reflect the problems of worldview of transition. Hence the need for a *consistent* worldview.

The mechanical and electromagnetic approaches to potential energy involve rather *different world views*. The epistemological project established by Newton and followers has the interactions between material bodies, the mechanics, as the main subject.

The world view based on electromagnetism, the framework proposed at the end of the nineteenth century, involves another epistemology.

The reality is that the charges are source of new reality, the fields, which acquire an autonomous "reality" and become *the conveyors of physical qualities*.[4] Thus there is an inversion in positions: things become 'upside down'. What has been accidental in the Newtonian (classical) world becomes general and common in the post-classical world and vice versa. What was general earlier becomes part of the new 'general'.

Engels, Lenin and a Critique of 'Speculative Materialism'

It is stated in a recent article[5], School of Languages and Cultures (University of Sydney) that already in the nineteenth century, "the debate between scientific materialists, historical materialists and neo-Kantians had a political component, restaging in important respects the Enlightenment conflict between faith and reason. While the scientific materialists broadly saw their work as undermining a reactionary theological worldview, their opponents despaired at the moral and political consequences of rejecting free will altogether. However, this debate would be replayed yet again in the twentieth century, with even wider-reaching political implications."[6]

This is an understatement. First of all, what has been termed as 'scientific materialists' were the natural scientists who delved into philosophical questions also. 'Scientific materialism' emerged in the consequence of developments in natural as well as social sciences. It cannot be reduced to 'politics', though a part of course concerned the social realities. It was reason that was strengthened as a result. In fact, the materialists successfully countered idealist and agnostic approaches. That was great contribution of Marxist and other materialists, and the great merit of dialectics by Hegel and others. The Marxist dialecticians continued the tradition of Hegel and thus made a fundamental contribution to the unveiling of the world. Frederick Engels has dealt with them very well in his *Dialectics of Nature* and other works.

The struggle between faith and reason also was not a mainly political struggle, as it unfolded the realities of the material world. It is also incorrect to suggest that this is being 'replayed' in the 20th or 21st centuries, because lot of original philosophical concepts are being worked out and reworked.

"For if neo-Kantian and Marxist materialists shared a certain skepticism concerning knowledge of the world as it is 'in itself', they were nevertheless also united by an ongoing commitment to the idea that such a world exists."[7]

It has to be said to the credit of dialectical materialists that they countered the Kantian arguments of 'thing-in-itself' and of agnosticism. They opposed the very concept of the 'thing-in-itself'. Thus they and the Kantians cannot be put in the same category.

"In the wake of neo-Kantianism, however, positivist thinkers such as the Austrian physicist Ernst Mach pushed the logic of Kant's critical epistemology to breaking point. Mach argued that '[w]hat we represent to ourselves behind the appearances exists *only* in our understanding', and has the value of an 'arbitrary and irrelevant [...] formula'. His critique of materialism was highly provocative, resting as it did on the assertion that 'the world consists only of our sensations'", "a claim that seemed to deny even the existence of a reality external to the human mind."[8] Here the author has rightly found a continuation of the Kantian agnosticism and 'thing-in-itself' in neo-Kantianism. Such a philosophy does not do justice to the new discoveries in electromagnetism and other fields. But then further on, criticism by Lenin on similar lines is sought to be undermined, deliberately forcing it to the 'power politics', and thus reducing its importance.

"Although Mach developed his critical empiricism largely in opposition to the materialism of the nineteenth century, in the early twentieth century his ideas became extremely popular" among those who were eager to keep abreast of the latest scientific developments. "Alexander Bogdanov in his book *Empirio-monism* (1904–06), attempted to combine Mach's philosophy of science with the materialist conception of history. Bogdanov believed that materialist philosophy had become too abstract, and that the empiriocriticism of Mach, Richard Avenarius and others had 'restored its sense', namely 'the physical complexes, how they are given in experience'". Bogdanov saw in Mach's work a useful theory of the role human subjectivity plays in shaping our knowledge of the external world.[9]

It has to be commented that this is strange way of combining philosophy of science with the materialist conception of history, as the subject and subjectivity are treated from the vantage point opposite that of the materialist conception.

Bogdanov also clearly believed that Mach's own perspective was limited, and that he had gone beyond it. He claimed he had taken 'only one' idea from Mach, namely that 'concerning the neutrality of elements of experience with respect to the "physical" and the "psychological", about the dependence of these characteristics only on the *connections* of experience'. Other than that, Bogdanov claimed to have 'nothing in common' with Mach.[10]

It was precisely the 'one idea' that Bogdanov did take from Mach that drew criticism from Vladimir Lenin. In his *Materialism and Empirio-Criticism,* Lenin showed that Bogdanov's theory amounted to claim that material reality is an imaginary product of the senses. Lenin argued, Bogdanov's work was fundamentally at odds with materialism.[11]

To be sure, Lenin 'agreed', as per the author of the article, that *matter* was a 'philosophical category'. Nevertheless, it was a category 'denoting the objective reality which is given to man by his sensations'. For what else could produce sensation if not 'matter acting upon our sense-organs'? asked Lenin.[12]

Lenin not only 'agreed' with the concept of the philosophical category of matter, he in fact actively developed it further. Lenin's recognition of matter as a concept went beyond that of the 'scientific materialists', for whom matter was still a 'universal material', as he, Lenin put it, detached from force. When Lenin argued, against the Machists, that matter is a 'philosophical category denoting the objective reality which is given to man', he explicitly saw himself as continuing in Engels's footsteps, as per the author.[13]

This is an intriguing way of putting things: Lenin 'seeing himself' in the footsteps of Engels! He in fact continued the latter's line of reasoning.

The author continues, however, "by reformulating the concept of matter to include the whole of 'objective reality' Lenin made the same error of which Engels accused the scientific materialists", who, he claimed, 'leave out of account the qualitative differences of things in lumping them together [...] under the concept matter'".[14] How? Engels also includes the objective reality in the concept of matter: objective reality is that which exists independent of our consciousness. So there is a lot of mix-up and jumbling of concepts while trying to criticize the precise concepts developed by Engels and Lenin. Engels also depicts the role of sense-perceptions in the formation of consciousness, and Lenin too in his abovementioned book.

Actually, this is what Engels says about matter: Matter is a pure creation of thought and an abstraction. Qualitative differences are left out of the concept. Hence matter is distinct from the definite, existing pieces of matter, and therefore "is not anything sensuously existing." Natural science does not seek out uniform matter.[15]

It is accused that by claiming that material reality is 'copied, photographed and reflected by our sensations, while existing independently of them', *Materialism and Empirio-criticism* neglected the role of consciousness in shaping our experience.[16]

How the role of consciousness is neglected by Lenin here is not at all clear. It is a very loose kind of criticism directed against him. As referred by the author herself, Lenin has clearly mentioned the role of perception in the formation of consciousness.

In fact, Engels and Lenin do not differ from each other on all these basic propositions.

Concept of Matter in Philosophy and Physics

New discoveries are being made in all the sciences, as also in the social sciences. But the discoveries in physics, more than in any other discipline, are causing controversies about the new world, raising fresh questions about philosophy and new worldview. Physics, of all the sciences, is opening up vistas of an entirely new world. We are passing from classical world to a new, postclassical world, thanks to discoveries about novel realities.

Dealing with the philosophical implications of discoveries in physics, we have to keep in mind that the concepts used in physics and philosophy overlap, *yet they are not the same.* Matter is a concept used both in physics and in philosophy. We should not get confused.

In philosophy, matter is a concept used to cover the whole of reality/existence, including the part we are yet to contact. Therefore, it is a *philosophical concept,* which we do not come into contact with physically; what we do come in contact with is the individual fields and expressions of matter, like rocks, trees, organisms including microorganisms, stars, planets and so on. Matter is used to denote *everything* that exists independent of us, particularly of our consciousness: everything minus consciousness, the very reality or existence. This applies more to the materialist or realist philosophies.

In physics, matter is the one that keeps coming across in the course of our life and investigations. It is generally a tangible 'thing', *distinct from, for example, energy*. It is the things we come in contact with, affecting our thoughts or consciousness. We do come in contact with forms of energy but that is when it is part of matter. We are not able to come in direct contact with energy as an independent entity.

The change in the nature of matter and space was noted in an interesting manner by Einstein: "Space is now turning round and eating up matter"![17]

Matter and energy are *two distinct* concepts and realities in physics. Sometimes they are even used inter-changeably.

In philosophy, *energy is part of the concept of matter,* just like any other object. In physics, energy is an entity separate from matter.

Therefore, we should be very careful when we come across the use of the word/concept of matter in physics and in philosophy. *They cannot be used interchangeably, only overlappingly.*

Physics reveals to us the realities, processes and phenomena in a particular field of reality, just as chemistry, biology, astronomy and other disciplines do. Natural sciences reveal the concrete features, laws, characteristics in various areas of existence. It is their totality that reveals the full picture.

Philosophy draws upon these discoveries to strengthen, revise or form its concepts. Sciences are the life sources of the generalizations about events happening in the various fields.

Yet certain developments in physics have affected our views about the world as a whole. Since the discoveries in electromagnetism, splitting of atom, quantum, relativity, etc, new features and structures of the world are emerging, which bring about a transformation in our worldview. This new picture does not fit in with the existing picture and concepts. Consequently, certain basic philosophical questions have been reopened. They include the nature of observation and the observed, causality, matter, matter-consciousness relations, nature of 'reality' and existence, formation of consciousness, subject-object relationship, nature of the 'new world', and many others.

Debates and discussions broke out soon after these discoveries, and continue unabated till now. There was severe philosophical discussion on the splitting of the atom and consequent nature of 'matter'. Some people including important scientists announced the 'death' or 'end of matter'. *This is partly because the concept of matter in physics is more limited compared to that in philosophy.*

Electromagnetism, quantum and relativity opened out series of debates on the nature of reality etc. A.S. Eddington wrote a detailed work on the nature of electron and of reality way back in 1927, published in 1929 as *The Nature of the Physical World.*[18]

Says Eddington, "Rutherford introduced the greatest change in our idea of matter since the time of Democritus.[19] He was dealing with the structure of the atom. He says something interesting further: "...when I hear today protests against the Bolshevism of modern science and regrets for the old-established order, I am inclined to think that Rutherford, not Einstein, is the real villain of the piece."[20]

Talking about the concept of atom and its philosophization, Eddington says "atom is as porous as the solar system."[21] This porosity is not presupposed in the atomic theory. At first solar system type of atom substituted for billiard type atom.[22] The old 'substantial atom' is unthinkable.[23] We have reached the limits of physical knowledge.[24] "No familiar conceptions can be woven round the electron: it belongs to the waiting list." It cannot just be 'tossed up'.[25] There are no 'bodies' on atomic scale; there are only 'probabilities' at that scale.[26]

Thus a revival of philosophical discussions took place in the first 2 or 3 decades of the 20th century itself.

There were three 'Solvay Congresses', named after the Belgian industrialist Ernest Solvay, who funded them and the Solvay Institutes. The first Solvay conference was held in 1911, and then was held fairly regularly. They were attended by the most outstanding scientists. For the example, out of 27 scientists attending the third Solvay conference, 16 were present or future Nobel laureates. Philosophical and other implications of the quantum and other discoveries inevitably came up for discussions.

Among the most celebrated debates was that between Einstein and Niels Bohr, which ran for some 35 years. We have dealt with it earlier. Among the main issues was whether there existed an independent objective reality or whether we influenced, even created it in the course of our observations.

'Death' of Materialism?

Some interesting problems have been discussed by Paul Davies and John Gribbin[27] on the nature of matter and materialism today. Industrial revolution was a time of triumph of materialism and of human confidence.

"Newton's view of matter as inert substance shaped and formed by external forces became deeply ingrained in Western culture."[28] Forces of nature were tamed in the 18th and 19th centuries. Clockwork and machine work became the basis of the worldview. Newtonian worldview with its clockwork view helped the development of sciences immensely. It simultaneously developed a machine-mindedness, and came to consider human beings as 'cogs' in the system of universe.

According to the authors, "It is fitting that physics—the science that gave rise to materialism—should also signal the demise of materialism."[29]

We need to discuss materialism here and also what is meant by its demise, and whether it really died? The authors mention discoveries of relativity, quantum and others as those having 'overthrown' materialism. The quantum totally transformed our image of matter. In the old assumption, the microscopic world was just a scaled down image of the Newtonian world of tangible solid objects. This picture was broken. It was now a world of waves and particles, governed by 'the rules of chance' rather than of causality.[30] Say the authors: "Quantum physics undermines materialism because it reveals matter has far less 'substance' than we might believe."[31]

The point here is that materialism of physics is identified with the world of the tangible and solid objects. It is this world, no doubt, that has disappeared with the discoveries of the EM, the quantum and the new particle. This does not mean that matter of philosophy has 'disappeared'. In fact the *philosophical matter* has been enriched. A particular form of matter, and materialism as a generalization of that 'matter', has definitely disappeared. But then matter exists as waves and particles of a different kind. After all, they are real forces, even when they are unknown before observation and are modified after observation. That is altogether a different point.

Physics no doubt contributed a lot to develop 'materialism' further. It did not 'give rise' to materialism but strengthened it. Materialism existed prior to physics or developed physics. It has been in existence in form of atomism of the ancient Greek or Indian philosophy. Materialism and philosophy are worldview in general, not simply of science or a branch of it. Sciences, physics included, no doubt strongly contribute to and strengthen materialism. They strengthen only materialism, not mysticism, obscurantism, agnosticism, *apriorism,* idealism, etc because they do not deny material reality but confirm it.

If you believe in agnosticism today, when the natural sciences have developed to a high degree, you only strengthen obscurantism by throwing back and denying all the development in scientific ideas. Scientific ideas and philosophy in general must keep updating themselves along with the sciences. If ideas fall back when sciences are developing, and if scientific ideas do not keep pace with the development of the sciences in general, they act as a drag on development of ideas and consciousness, even on scientific consciousness.

Newton's laws and *Newtonianism* have greatly contributed to and confirmed materialism and dialectics. "Newton's image of matter as inert lumps"[32] was a physical view, not a philosophical view. If we confuse physical view with philosophical view and identify them both, certainly there is 'end of matter'! But this is not so. It is the 'end of the inert matter', not of matter itself.

Matter is a concept, a philosophical category, covering or encompassing the entire existence outside our consciousness, as objective reality not dependent on our ideas. Our ideas merged later, matter was in existence before. "Matter' can be an inert lump *and* an active microorganism or wave/particle duality.

The discovery of electromagnetism filled the gap between the 'inert lumps' of tangible objects, and thus imparted new dimensions to the concept of matter. It extends the concept of matter. EM showed the unity of the 'inert lumps' and fast moving waves and particles in the field and space. The two are entirely two kinds of qualitatively different material forms. So much so that the laws of one do not apply to the other. In fact the EM has taken for the first time deeper into an entirely new world or existence.

This world does exist, only it exists not as we presume or expect.

Philosophy had at least two functions to discharge during the mechanical, industrial age. With the help of various sciences, it delved deeper into matter and its forms. Philosophy has been a speculative science. At the same time it is 'science of sciences'. Industrial and mechanics revolution provided it proofs of speculations, turning them into reality. Its hypotheses and concepts changed from speculations to concrete truths. That is why philosophy is sometimes confused with concrete sciences. It is a world outlook or world view, which includes the view of the whole 'world' as it exists, and also of what does not exist. To view the world one necessarily turns to materialism, consciously or unconsciously. There is nothing mystic in it all. Therefore it is surprising and regrettable as well that some of the scientists revert back to mysticism, *apriorism* and agnosticism. A world which is post-classical cannot be explained using the laws of pre-industrial, pre-scientific era.

On the other hand resorting to pragmatism and positivism is nothing other than reductionism, an attempt to limit sciences and philosophy to the surface and 'apparent' events. Development of the natural sciences was immense steps into the processes deep inside the surface of material processes.

They are materialism, yet not 'materialism'. The scientific approach definitely considers existence of objects independent of our ideas and consciousness. An objectively existing reality is essential for scientific investigations. Speculation or idea-forming is not enough for sciences. Science and scientific approach presuppose existence of reality.

The 'reality' consists of so many realities or parts, each studied by separate sciences. These realities are studied in their change and motion. In the earth conditions, the motions and changes and slow. The matter is laid back kind and 'existing' for certain period of time, for certain interval: you can come back to it tomorrow, day after and so on. So there is certain succession of events and order.

Here comes the role of dialectics and dialectical method. Dialectics uncovers the inner conflict and sources of motion. Mechanical motion is also dialectical in a sense. We often interpret mechanical laws in a 'mechanical, not dialectical, way. *Laws of motion are always dialectical.*

And here we come to the second function discharged by philosophy, that of discovering motion, whether of matter or of idea or of both. This is not strictly a philosophical function, yet philosophy necessarily moves into the field of motions and changes. Each of the sciences, whether natural or social, ultimately deal with the changes in their respective fields. Without recognition of change, discoveries cannot be made. Discovery means a recognition of motion and movement.

In the earthly conditions, the motions are slow, comparatively speaking. Recognition of motion and discovery of laws of motion are attempts to bring about an order and inter-connection in the world.

In biology motions in body and over whole historical epochs are dealt with. They are orderly and successive.

In chemistry, changes are between fixed structures of molecules, atoms, and elements etc. Molecules etc too have evolved over millennia, such as amino acids and proteins.

Physics dealt with motions of heat, light, gases, work, steam, etc. Newton organized the world into and through laws of motion of bodies, both heavenly and earthly. They may appear to be mechanical today, but they were highly dialectical, because after the initial 'push', they kept moving on their own.

Every process had its own 'dialectics'. It is through inner conflict, change, giving up the old and acquiring the new, establishing new aspects and inter-connections that the processes and things evolved. Dialectical methodology tried to discover the sources of such motions, such as in biology or physics. A 'dialectics of nature' evolved, however much one may disagree with the approach.

Industrial revolution and its results laid much stress on the motions of the bodies, such as the machines. They were termed 'mechanical', which is true to some extent. They were repetitive and circular. But nothing can be really repetitive and circular; it must move out or move in closing or opening circles, that is move along spiral path. A mechanical machine seemingly is mechanical but in reality is changing, and therefore is dialectical.

Machine is a unity of different parts, which have each their own mechanics not exactly matching that of the other parts, yet matching in totality. Friction, for example, is very good example of dialectics in operation. It is one of the forces within the system, overcoming which the machine moves forward.

The development of the machine, historically, is itself a great example of dialectical development and evolution of the machine. There is conflict and unity between the main body, the tool and the motive power, as also between different parts, which need updating at certain points in historical development, so that the 'drawback' of the machine system is overcome and it goes ahead smoothly along.

Machines led to the rise of a mechanical view of things, of the processes on the earth and in the skies. Everything was seen in the fashion of machines, as has been rightly pointed out in many of the works, including of Davies and Gribbin.

In and under the impression of such a view, the world was seen as a giant machine working with mechanical laws. Classical physics is based on mechanical laws, yet it discovered dialectical laws, that is, laws of motion and change.

Motion is always 'is and is not'. The great German philosopher, the giant among the philosophers, Georg Hegel, was master of *dialectics,* and of dialectical method. He went into the very essence of things and phenomena and processes and uncovered their inner workings, their inner mechanism of dialectics. He really developed dialectics as a science. He dealt with motions of the *concept* and *the being*. Hegel belonged to an era when there was no electromagnetism and quantum. Yet he came very near this kind of reality through sheer use of *methodology of dialectics*. He almost identified himself with instant changes and transformations. His dialectics is of the highest order, and *fully applicable in the post-classical era of physics* of instant changes.

Classical physics deals with concepts of matter and motion, but they have an area of operation. They contribute to the general philosophical concepts by enriching what is universal. Yet matter and motion are concrete entities/ concepts in physics. They are not philosophical abstractions separate from concrete matter. Matter in philosophy is not a concept but a reality. Therefore it is not subject to the laws and categories of philosophy.

Consequently, a sudden change in the established nature of matter will not end the *philosophical matter,* it cannot signal the 'demise of matter'. It signals only the demise of 'particular' matter, or more correctly *material form.* Such a 'demise' unleashes new features of matter, which may be exactly opposite of those hitherto existing. Since matter in physics is a particular category, it reveals ever new features. *Since matter in philosophy is an abstraction, a concept, it constantly gets enriched and moves forward with the discoveries in physics.*

In fact, matter in philosophy and in concrete sciences, in some senses, are *two opposite poles*. They are the poles of the abstract and the concrete, one enriching the other, both mutually interpenetrating, yet never becoming one. They are 'one' or unity in the incompleteness of the other. Confusing the two would only complicate the matter, the issue, and lead to agnosticism and reductionism. Science is never reductionism and isolationism.

Philosophy has to be based on the *generalizations* of the scientific discoveries. The moment it ceases to generalize, it ceases to be philosophy. Engels was right to state in *Anti-Duhring* and *Dialectics of Nature* that philosophy ended where concrete sciences took over the job of discovering concrete realities. Since concrete scientific facts came to the fore, speculation became superfluous.

Both philosophy and dialectics, or the science of motion, developed during the industrial age. Mechanics is the product of machine revolution. It concretized the tangible objects, their motion and the laws of motion. Mechanical motion is dialectics in mechanical form.

In physics mechanics is the motion of tangible bodies, the 'inert lumps', but this motion is not 'mechanical'. The motion is not only between two or more bodies. Each inert body has its own independent source of motion. Earth has its own complicated *motion of motions*.

In philosophy, mechanical motion is repetitive and circular, without contributing to the system's further development. It is reduction of the general trend of motion.

Problem with philosophy and cognition today: The problem with consciousness today is that it is dealing with a qualitatively new kind of speed, conversions/transformations and reality. In the process, 'matter' is converted into matter with *'non-matter' features*. Things, and later our consciousness, have evolved in the conditions of gradual slowdown of time and matter. It is only through a slowdown that the earth and other planets of the solar system have emerged from the spheres of gases. Further slowdown has led to the evolution of liquids, solids, rocks, oceans and so on. The life forms then emerged. They evolved into the apes, who then evolved into human beings and their society. Emergence of humans led to the evolution of consciousness.

So our consciousness has evolved in conditions of orderly stage-wise development, in 'natural conditions'. The abovementioned events are natural, lead to natural developments. 'Nature' evolved on the earth, or earth is 'natural'. We and are our consciousness are product of this very nature. It is a slow-motion development, where things and processes are well ordered, disciplined, clearly placed, with their respective places well-known, one evolving or emerging out of the other. This development, these motions have their own laws of motion, change and development. They are discovered and explained by the respective sciences, natural and social.

Things are different in the world of electromagnetism, quantum and relativity. There is a certain order but of a faint kind. One changes into another instantly: a particle can change into waves, which simultaneously keep particles popping out. The particles keep popping out of and disappearing into 'space' all the time, and waves swish past in no time all the time! Fields and forces are being created, disappearing the next instant or changing into something else. All this happens at light speed or near it, totally destabilizing and destroying both the object and the subject.

It is the speed up of events. Therefore, time is the determining factor in this reality, even while it ceases to exist in the earthly, natural, usual sense.

Even though the industrial revolution speeded up time/

development, it remained within the 'natural' limits. There has been certain 'speeding up' of evolution of the earth the last few millennia and centuries. But things remained within the limits of orderly conversions and evolution. Hence the different kinds of 'laws' help us understand matter and material forms.

Things changed drastically and qualitatively since the discovery of electromagnetism, quantum and relativity, as also some others. The 'atom' has disappeared, and along with it the constituent particles and sub-particles. Both waves and particles have become highly problematic. They do not fit in with the picture of the constituting elements or particles of nature. By extending our natural philosophy, we tried to explain the world by constituting it with the help of 'basic' building blocks, in the manner that the bricks constitute the building.

This is where our consciousness slipped. What suddenly appeared before us with the EM is a world without 'building blocks'. We are not used to such a world; we cannot imagine a 'world' which has no building blocks, the basic units of which the whole world and its things are made of. The 'order', the basic structure is gone! Therefore the very basis of our concepts, of our ideas and consciousness has disappeared!! We have to find new basis or bases. But the new basis that is emerging is highly 'slippery', unstable, disappearing all the time, changing too quickly, converting all the time. It is world of energy conversions, wherein matter has 'disappeared', so to say! Therefore we cannot form our concept. The concepts too must move at light speed, and therefore they are no concepts at all!

It is a crisis, a historical crisis, a crisis of our very existence, a crisis of the existence of our consciousness itself. How do we form our consciousness if we are not able to 'see', even with the latest equipments? The equipments themselves are industrial, made up of the industrial materials, and therefore they 'favor' the industrial processes. We are increasingly using unnatural 'things' like the rays and light etc in these equipments, but that creates further confusion. The moment we use equipments made of natural and industrial material, they unite and conflict with the sub-atomic processes and create new realities. Thus we encounter novel reality.

Materials and speeds inside the atom had so far no role in the evolution of our consciousness. Now is the point of crisis. So far we evolved as 'Part One' of history, the only part so far. Now, it seems, we have just entered 'Part Two'. Consciousness was all powerful, based upon this prolonged development of hundreds of thousands of years. All that is undone now, in a matter of few years only. We now find that the laws we discovered and evolved are unable to explain the new realities. There is a huge qualitative change now. The unnatural forces are being unleashed. They do not fit in with the existing realities based on matter and ideas. We find that matter and ideas now coalesce, interpenetrate, form one reality.

The new reality is based on exceedingly rapid conversions. It is conversions only, that too at high speeds, at near light and light speeds. How can consciousness form in such circumstances, in circumstances where nothing 'is there', and everything 'is not there'! In fact there is no 'thing'. The 'thing' was the very basis of our consciousness, which now has been dragged away from under the consciousness like a magical carpet! What shall consciousness do? Where should it look for the 'thing'?

What is 'out there' now? What are object and objectivity? These and other questions, dealt by philosophy, have re-emerged. What is out there is not clear, because nothing really exists as and in 'now'. The moment we try to grasp the out there, it transforms into something else. There is no doubt something is out there. In that sense objectivity is there. But it is beyond consciousness, in the sense that as soon as we try to grasp it, it changes. So we are unable to see the 'original' (!), because the original is undergoing utterly rapid conversions. What we see there is the result of the interaction between consciousness and the 'out there'. It is the future we should all the time be looking for, not the present.

The 'reality' is becoming part of our consciousness in real terms.

"The more science moves away from common sense, the harder it is to decide what constitutes... the real world."[33] We increasingly take recourse to calculations, mathematical suppositions, probabilities etc to determine the nature of what exists or 'is there'. What is being described is the change and conversions.

In the 1930s, physicists were deeply influenced by 'positivism', a philosophical movement "which seeks to root reality only in what can actually be observed."[34] At that time, Niels Bohr, Heisenberg and others argued that when we talk of atoms, electrons and others, "we must not fall into the trap of imagining them as little 'things'" existing independently,[35] the word 'atom' is a sort of consistent logical system relating different observations, which are connected through mathematical algorithm. So positivism lost 'ground'!

It is all a description of an abstract concept in physical *language*.

It does not mean that the *atom* is really 'out there', a well-defined entity with all the possible fixed features. It has no definite location in space and definite velocity through space. Heisenberg says: "...but the atoms or the elementary particles themselves are not as real; they form a world of potentialities or possibilities rather than one of things or facts."[36]

Says Niels Bohr: Physics is not about how the world *is*, it is about what we can *say* about the world."[37]

Changed Concept of Matter

Electromagnetism and quantum have changed our concept of matter, in physical sense, and considerably in the philosophical sense. This needs serious and well-considered discussion. We should be prepared for drastic changes in the world view and should not be tied to the concepts of the past.

The microscopic world is not a scaled down picture of everyday Newtonian view. Quantitative changes lead to qualitative ones. When we reached the stage of the new kind of particle, we found it inseparably linked to and intertwined with the cloud or the waves. In fact, particle turns out convert itself into wave when we try to analyze it. We enter a new world, governed by waves and particles govern the new world.

It has inaugurated the era of *information revolution,* which imparts new aspects to the process of cognition. It is claimed by George Gilder that this constitutes an 'overthrow of matter' and an ascendancy of power of mind. This is a transformation of a material world of inert particles into a radiant world of sparks of informative energy.[38]

Here there is a clear mix-up of 'matter' of physics with the matter of philosophy. The former is 'dead', the latter is enriched.

Not everything in the classical world is 'inert particles'. The whole biological evolution and existence is lively. Besides, 'information' is not existence, it is use. Science is transformed into information technology, which uses processes existing independently into those consumable by us. So information is use of an objective process. They are not exclusive to each other, although they constitute the opposite poles of the same process. Human/computer and brain/computer interface are the example of the dialectical opposites and their inter-penetration and growing merger.

There is no 'overthrow of matter', otherwise there would not be so much physical and philosophical discussions in science over the nature of matter. The point is that the nature of matter has changed, it has not disappeared, it has become invisible, 'difficult to catch', and has to be reached via probabilities and potentialities. These are two different kinds of speeds at work, creating cognitive problems for the brain and the consciousness. At the same time, as the experiments in brain/computer interface show, brain (matter) is nearing the exceedingly rapid processes of waves and 'particles'; it is becoming *unnecessary* for the physical processes to move via biophysical structures. They can take recourse to the electronic systems. New bio-physical and bio-electronic systems are emerging. Brains can see and think and make changes on the screen. Thinking is seeing, seeing is thinking. A process of merger has set in. This is a new stage in the evolution of matter and consciousness.

These developments extend the matter instead of overthrowing it. At the same time, they bring matter nearer to consciousness, and resolve idea, thought and consciousness into the levels of matter, the material world, which is momentary and rapid. Processes of brain/consciousness are merging with those of the new stages of matter being discovered, beginning with electromagnetism, quantum and so on.

It will be erroneous to state that 'matter has disappeared'. It will be more correct that study of matter has reached a point, a level of matter has been discovered, where brain/consciousness identify more easily with matter. At this level we interact with matter increasingly by changing and modifying it. We are unable to state in what state matter is before observation. We definitely are able to state the result of our interaction with the waves, particles, their dualities and motions.

It is a new kind of interaction between matter consciousness/brain.

EM and other discoveries is enabling us to live in a world of information emanating from new and deeper levels of material processes.

Davies and Gribbin make crucial point when they state that we live "a network of forces and fields."[39] They also make another crucial point that the new social order will be based upon not on the clockwork image of Newtonian materialism, but on the network image of the post-Newtonian world view.[40] only, we should be clear, this 'post-Newtonian world view' is not based on the disappearance of matter but on enrichment of the concept of matter.

Electromagnetic Worldview

We have given some indications about it in the course of the book. In the book we have basically stuck to the field of electromagnetism, and not dealt much with other discoveries.

Among the most important features of the problem is that electromagnetism is a wide range of waves, mostly invisible. We are habituated during our history to its visible part in form of light. It is light which so far fashioned our view of the world, without us being aware of it or of the nature of light. Therefore the theoretical possibility opens up of the existence of a world constituted by these waves and their wave-lengths, which is not lighted. What kind of world is this, we do not know. Even about lighted world we know very little. The lighted world constitutes only about 4 percent of 'reality', the rest 96 percent is without light.

Light travels so fast, at 3 lakh km/sec, that we are unaware of it, and find it is all the time 'there'!

This is one aspect. The second aspect is really important. *Till electromagnetism was discovered*, the world constituted of tangible objects moving at certain speeds in time and in space. The dialectics of it is complicated, stage-wise and layer by layer, and this crucial feature has to be kept in mind.

Between two or more tangibles, there existed empty spaces, as we have mentioned several times. Discovery of electromagnetism filled up that space. But it filled it up in a most *unexpected* way: it has completely transformed the relationship between the tangible and the intangible realities. Fields, forces, electrons, charges, etc filled up this space. They neither move in relation to the space nor in relation to a fixed time. And they move at very high speeds. They become independent, sovereign entities. The 'fixed time' ended here.

What is our direct relation to the phenomena like fields, forces and charges? It is difficult to establish such a relation. We relate now to the 'object' in high motion, which is changing and transforming all the time, and practically disappears in no time. Higgs boson 'exists' for billionth of a millionth of a second! This is the reality of which the existing reality made. Most unstable reality constitutes the stable tangibles. This is the dialectical contradiction of objectivity as well as of subjectivity. Besides, the object is not tangible; therefore the concept 'object' is difficult to apply here. There is nothing fixed or stable. We are habituated to relate with objects with a certain life and stability. That is how the subject-object relationship is created in the earthly conditions.

It is obvious that in order to relate with fields, forces and electromagnetic waves, we have to take recourse to indirect means or routes. We have to convert them into certain formulas, mathematical points and calculations, which give us an approach to some picture of 'reality', to which we then relate. This reality is complex and complicated. It is clear that one cannot relate with waves and charged particles as with normal objects. So it is their picture or formula that we treat to uncover the reality.

The concept of 'matter' undergoes serious revision and transformation. While matter continues to be objective and existing independently of our consciousness, it is not possible for us to relate with it or for it to be reflected in our consciousness. To be reflected, it needs to be transformed through a series of changes to enable it to be digested by our consciousness system. It is a growing conflict of the speeded up reality with our consciousness.

"Matter i.e. substance and field, is not, on the whole, particles or waves in the sense of classical theories...Particle and wave properties are united in their opposition. In other words, matter simultaneously has the properties of particles and waves."[41]

Charged electrons and particles moving at near light speeds need to be caught on the apparatuses and calculated to enable us to grasp. Normally we are not aware of the speeds of electrons and light. But with the present speeding up through technology, we are discovering how matter is constituted at these speeds. Now we can get a feel of the light speed. But then we move away from the tangible realities. In the process they modified considerably. It is the modified object/s that we 'observe'. We do not know their nature exactly before observation. This is a key epistemological problem of the observation of the world constituted of the waves and particles.

EM waves are waves that are created as a result of vibrations between an electric field and a magnetic field. This is how the energy is transported around us in the world. They do not require a medium in contrast to the mechanical waves.

In an indirect relationship, we try to catch the world at dizzying speeds; they disappear or appear in modified forms. The empty spaces are full of motions and forms most unfamiliar to us. It is a new reality, which stands redefined. It is the first time we are forced to speed up ourselves in order to grasp the new realities, to move with their speeds and velocities.

What is reality now? It is clear that it is not enough to state that matter exists independently of our consciousness. That will be *inadequate*. We have to go through innumerable steps to reach the reality of light speed and waves/particles at that speed. A world of energy transformations opens up before us. Nothing is stationary and fixed and in shape in that world. The slightest touch or 'interference' disturbs that waves and particles in that world. Particles are not fixed but exceedingly momentary formations or result of wave coincidences or quantum ejection. "The concept of observability (or non-observability) should not in fact be applied to the wave function as such: the latter is a *mathematical* quantity, while observability concept applies only the *physical*."[42]

Dialectics and New Worldview

The other crucial aspect of the new discoveries is the greater importance of dialectics of the events and the method of dialectics itself. The world of electromagnetism can only be grasped if the method of dialectics is used properly. Dialectics means change, and it is change *at dizzying speeds* in this part of reality. Processes are exceedingly momentary, and therefore the consequent concepts have also to be momentary and transitory. Since the existence is disappearing all the time, it becomes difficult to talk of an object; in fact there are no 'objects' as such. Everything is process and conversion. We have to talk of them only as motion, not matter or material things.

So it is dialectics par excellence! We can virtually 'see' dialectics in operation. This can be seen in connection with the whole range of electromagnetic waves, both visible and non-visible, both before the infra-red and beyond the ultra-violet. Earlier we had to search for it laboriously. Conflicts, opposites, mutual conversion of the opposites, qualitative and quantitative changes, constant negation, and so on had to be step by step worked out and discovered through painstaking researches and detailed study. This is true even now, but we can really see these 'things' happening. They are constantly taking place. Entry into the new world of rapid motions is a confirmation of dialectics. Hegel and other dialecticians become ever more relevant. Dialectics has to be mastered.

It is world of constant dialectics in ever-changing matter.

It was earlier thought that the "energetic world within the atom that lay beyond the scope of gravitation or electromagnetism"[43] was *safe from interference from 'outside'*. This is a crucial practical and philosophical question. The point is that in a tangible and mechanistic world (why do we consider the world always mechanistic? Why do we lose sight of dialectics?!), there is a direct interference in the material processes. These processes and things are inter-related. One thing or process is always based upon something else. But in the world of electromagnetism and quantum, they are *not based upon anything*. They are independent entities. Therefore the possibilities of outside interference is much less or none at all. The 'outside' here is the classical world.

The forces inside the objects are, so to say, 'protected' from 'outside' forces. In a chemical compound for example, there are elements, molecules and compounds. They are composed of atoms. The changes in the elements and molecules do not affect or change the processes within the atom. They are protected. The release of forces within the atom may lead to a reactor or a bomb. That is how they behave on the earth.

To work with each level of force, e.g. biological, chemical, physical, geological, etc, we must unleash the working of forces and energy within each level. The energy transformations within the atom are neither affected by gravitation, electromagnetism, mechanical or chemical or biochemical etc forces. Each has its own domain. It is the job of the process of cognition to unveil the forces and energy transformation within each level. These forces keep the object in shape, which we cognize in and through our theory of knowledge.

The relationship with us therefore is direct, one to one and object-subject kind.

In the post-classical world, the energy and forces are released as electromagnetism and quantum etc. They acquire an independent existence. We cannot establish direct, one to one and subject-object kind of relation with them. The moment we try to do so, the moment we 'interfere', the process changes. In the earthly conditions, they are 'protected', and so do not change in the process of observation. In case of 'post-natural reality', our interference changes it, and we encounter the result of observation, not the process/object itself. So we need to assess the extent and nature of interference and then conclude about the nature of the object, *the probability*. Instead of the object, it is the *probability of the object* that is important. We move from the domain of the fixed objects and motions to that of the continuous motions and conversions. We have to make final entry into the world of the probability and instability, and moving with them will give better view.

Our philosophical approach undergoes qualitative change at high velocities. Worldview and philosophy move in time determination and with time, increasingly losing the tangibility of the object and objective processes. We have to pose questions about transformations, conversions and amorphous nature of matter rather than about matter and reality itself. We are forced to think what and how to describe reality, rather than the exact nature of reality.

While Einstein consistently defends realism and objectivity, there is a problem. He seems to depart from the events of the quantum world. It is necessary today to establish a consistency of transition from the tangible to the intangible world, from classical to post-classical and from material world and materialism to 'un-material' world and a kind of materialism that continues materialism while denying and negating the mechanical tendencies and absorbing the realities seemingly inconsistent with 'materialism'.

Now we are fast delving into a world which is not 'given', not 'as it is'; it is a world which is not, which is all the time ceases to exist, and all the time disappearing into the future and is becoming all the time. It is not a physical but a 'relational' system. This new world is made of moments. We are all the time being immersed into a world of interactions and independent forces.

Our observation and conclusions depend on our velocities and frames of reference. If we speed up, our conclusions will change and observations will be different.

Bitbol says that according to Rovelli, the quantum state

is not a characteristic of physical systems but a relational characteristic that depends on the position of the observer during the process of knowledge acquisition. According to Olivier Rey, the paradoxes of quantum theory disappear if we accept that it is not "a science of the world as it is, but of the way we interact with it."[44]

Reality and Matter in the New World

There is no doubt we have now entered a world which is no more classical but is post-classical. How to we look at the 'reality' and 'matter' in such a world? The concepts of reality and matter, and our relation with them have become far more indirect and complicated.

The new reality is to be *derived* through a number of approaches, possibilities and probabilities. It is a reality which moving far more rapidly for us to grasp easily and directly. It is moving too fast to be comfortable for us. It is world where the laws, categories and concepts of the classical world simply collapse. We are connecting with the new world through the existing tools, mental and physical, which are inadequate or not applicable at all. When we apply the tangible tools, they interact with new reality at the latter's level, bringing about a change in it. The tools practically interact at the intangible levels, upsetting our expectations. Therefore, it is clear that the tools cannot take us into that world.

It is a reality of rapid energy conversions, of increasing complexity and deeper levels of wave/particle duality. Electromagnetism is a world of exceedingly rapid conversions of electric charges and fields. The tangible world practically plays no role at that level.

Such a world exists independent of our consciousness, is therefore part and parcel of the philosophical concept of matter. Since it affects our subjectivity in novel ways, it is object and objectivity with novelties. Our consciousness is fashioned in ways most unprecedented. The role of the material processes at quantum levels is enhanced as never before. These processes are at the same time mental and subjective. The base of idea formation is shifting to rapid transformations, becoming more akin to brain-like processes.

Mental and Physical Poles

The relationship between the mental and physical realities/poles has reached interesting phase with the EM and quantum mechanics. Without going into details, we will outline only some emerging features. We can say on the basis of scientific theories and experiments being conducted that the two processes are merging mutually. What we experience as mind may move the body by reaching the level of its quantum potential and affecting the motions of the particles/waves.[45] Brain/computer interface experiments also point in this direction. We have briefly discussed it in Chapter 7.

According to Bohm and Hiley, the content of our consciousness is becoming part of this process, and it is implied that a rudimentary mind-like quality exists at the level of particle physics. At each level of reality, there is a mental pole and a physical one. Thus even an electron has 'mental pole', rudimentary of course, represented mathematically by quantum potential[46], as mentioned earlier. These poles cannot be reduced to mere functions of each other, as is done in idealism and materialism.

Classical physics reflected only the objective structure of the human being as the observer, with no room for the mental process. The latter was considered as separate or just a part of the material reality.[47]

But now an observation of even the subtle mental processes of the observer can be made. The observer is not separate from larger reality. The larger reality is reflected on and reacts with the subtle mental processes as wave-particle duality. "...through the human being, the universe is making a mirror to observe itself."[48] In other words, the wave-particle duality of the universe reacts with that in our mind. This of course is unconscious process, and no conscious being or idea is involved, and so no mystic conclusions should be drawn.

The human/computer and brain/computer interfaces are opening new areas of interaction of 'matter and idea'. Matter is acquiring more mind-like features and idea is proving to be directly related to material changes. Thinking can be reduced to electromagnetic processes, which can be converted into letters and images. It is being proved that '*thought is material*'.

It is becoming clearer that quantum mechanics is not a representation *of* the world but of our position *in* the world. As Einstein famously stated: '*Time and space are modes by which we think, not conditions in which we live*'.[49]

For example, we see lighted objects but not the speed of light. We can see and feel the speed of all other objects.

While the reality exists objectively and matter has been in existence even before emergence of consciousness, this reality and this form of matter require new categories, laws and concepts to grasp them. Becoming part of the post-classical world, we need new approaches and new processes of cognition.

Human being, consciousness and subject-object relationship is drastically transforming itself in the post-classical reality. We become part of a world where our position and frame of reference and motion determine our being. The more our consciousness and existence become part of EM world, quantum and relativity, the more we will be able to grasp that world and define our existence and consciousness. Philosophy has to evolve where it can negotiate the new realities.

We enter a new post-classical world full of unprecedented novelties. Let us explore it.

NOTES

1. Based on Reubil, Karam, Gurgel and Robilotta, "Electromagnetism as a worldview: implications for the teaching of

energy", *Revista Brasileira de Ensino de F´ısica*, Vol. 39, No. 4, e4311, 2017 (www.scielo.br/rbef).

2. Ibid.
3. Ibid.
4. Ibid.
5. Cat Moir, "In Defence of Speculative Materialism", *Historical Materialism*, 2018 (1-33), School of Languages and Cultures, University of Sydney.
6. Ibid, p. 22.
7. Ibid.
8. Ibid.
9. Ibid, p. 23.
10. Ibid.
11. V.I. Lenin, *Materialism and Empirio-criticism*, Chapter 4, Section 5 on A Bogdanov's 'Empirio-monism'.
12. V.I. Lenin, *Materialism and Empirio-criticism.*
13. Cat Moir, p. 24.
14. Ibid, p. 24.
15. Engels, *Anti-Duhring*, PPH, New Delhi, 2011, p. 430.
16. Moir, p. 24.
17. V.S. Barabeshkov, "The Laws of the General Relativity Theory and the Phenomena of the Microworld", in, *Einstein and the Philosophical Problems of 20th Century Physics*, Progress Publishers, Moscow, 1979, p. 328.
18. A.S. Eddington, *The Nature of the Physical World*, 1929.
19. Ibid, p. 1.
20. Ibid.
21. Ibid.
22. Ibid, p. 2.
23. Ibid, p. 3.
24. Ibid, p. 257.
25. Ibid, p. 290.
26. Ibid, p. 305.
27. Paul Davies and John Gribbin, *The Matter Myth: Dramatic Discoveries that Challenge Our Understanding of Physical Reality*, Simon & Schuster Paperbacks, 2007.

28. Ibid, p. 11.
29. Ibid, p. 14.
30. Ibid.
31. Ibid.
32. Ibid, p. 15.
33. Ibid, p. 21.
34. Ibid, p. 27,
35. Ibid.
36. Ibid.
37. Ibid, emphasis in the original.
38. Ibid, p. 16.
39. Ibid, p. 17.
40. Ibid.
41. M.E. Omelyanovsky, *Dialectics in Modern Physics,* Progress Publishers, Moscow, 1979, p. 133.
42. Ibid, p. 100.
43. Paul Davies, *About Time: Einstein's Unfinished Revolution*, 1996, p. 14.
44. Interview given in *The Quantum World: Philosophical Debates on Quantum Physics,* edited by B. D'Espanat and H. Zwirn, 2017, p. 31-32.
45. See, D. Bohm and B.J. Hiley, *The Undivided Universe,* Routledge, 1993, p. 386.
46. Ibid, p. 387.
47. Ibid, p. 389.
48. Ibid.
49. Peter Atkins, *Galileo's Finger,* Oxford University Press, 2003, p. 275.

Index